Media Resistance

Trine Syvertsen

Media Resistance

Protest, Dislike, Abstention

Trine Syvertsen
Department of Media
 and Communication
University of Oslo
Oslo, Norway

ISBN 978-3-319-46498-5   ISBN 978-3-319-46499-2 (eBook)
DOI 10.1007/978-3-319-46499-2

Library of Congress Control Number: 2017930699

© The Editor(s) (if applicable) and The Author(s) 2017. This book is an open access publication.
Open Access This book is licensed under the terms of the Creative Commons Attribution 4.0 International License (http://creativecommons.org/licenses/by/4.0/), which permits use, sharing, adaptation, distribution and reproduction in any medium or format, as long as you give appropriate credit to the original author(s) and the source, provide a link to the Creative Commons license and indicate if changes were made.
The images or other third party material in this book are included in the book's Creative Commons license, unless indicated otherwise in a credit line to the material. If material is not included in the book's Creative Commons license and your intended use is not permitted by statutory regulation or exceeds the permitted use, you will need to obtain permission directly from the copyright holder.
The use of general descriptive names, registered names, trademarks, service marks, etc. in this publication does not imply, even in the absence of a specific statement, that such names are exempt from the relevant protective laws and regulations and therefore free for general use.
The publisher, the authors and the editors are safe to assume that the advice and information in this book are believed to be true and accurate at the date of publication. Neither the publisher nor the authors or the editors give a warranty, express or implied, with respect to the material contained herein or for any errors or omissions that may have been made. The publisher remains neutral with regard to jurisdictional claims in published maps and institutional affiliations.

Cover illustration: © Melisa Hasan

Printed on acid-free paper

This Palgrave Macmillan imprint is published by Springer Nature
The registered company is Springer International Publishing AG
The registered company address is: Gewerbestrasse 11, 6330 Cham, Switzerland

Acknowledgements

I am grateful to friends and colleagues who have inspired and challenged my ideas on media resistance. I am particularly indebted to Gunn Enli, Faltin Karlsen, Gro Bjørnerud Mo, Espen Ytreberg and Arild Aspøy, who have read and commented on the entire manuscript, as well as Ole Mjøs, Hallvard Moe and Vilde Schanke Sundet who have read many chapters. I truly appreciate your willingness to discuss overarching issues as well as sharing specific insights on topics relevant to the book.

Lene Vibeke Hansen and Chimen Darbandi have contributed valuably as research assistants. I am particularly grateful to Lene for her work in the early stages and to Chimen for her assistance on chapters 3, 4 and 5. Many colleagues have offered suggestions on specific topics; special thanks go to Jon Inge Faldalen for his film recommendations. I am also grateful to Dag Asbjørnsen and Siss Vik for encouraging me to write the book and their unfaltering interest in media protest and dislike.

The Faculty of Humanities and the Department of Media and Communications, University of Oslo, have provided me with research assistants as well as research leave, and an inspirational environment that has been invaluable to the project. The Open Access Funds at University and Department levels have covered the publication fee. I am also grateful to editors at Palgrave and their reviewers for tremendously useful feedback.

A final thanks go to all those who have shared their dislike of the media with me over the years, for inspiration and spirited exchange.

Contents

1 Media Resistance: Connecting the Dots   1

2 Resistance to Early Mass Media   15

3 Evil Media in Dystopian Fiction   35

4 "Get a Life!" Anti-Television Agitation and Activism   55

5 "Caught in the Net": Online and Social Media Disappointment and Detox   77

6 What if Resisters were Right? Speculations about Bad Media in Popular Films   99

7 Conclusion: The Persistence of Media Resistance   119

Bibliography   133

Index   147

CHAPTER 1

Media Resistance: Connecting the Dots

Abstract The chapter introduces the analysis of media resistance and presents the research questions: What is at stake for resisters, how did media resistance inspire organized action and how is media resistance sustained? Media resisters are often seen as moralists, Luddites, laggards or cultural pessimists, but this book argues that media resistance is grounded in broadly shared values: Morality, culture, enlightenment, democracy, community and health.

Keywords Media resistance · Luddite · Laggards · Moral panic · Media panic

Growing up Without Television

I grew up without television. My parents believed that television was a bad thing; it cost too much, would take attention away from other activities, would lead to passivity and obstruct family life. This was in Norway in the 1960s and my parents' beliefs resonated with the dominant misgivings about television at the time.

As a child, I was proud of our TV-free life. But the resistance did not stick. I moved in with others who had television. I did media studies in the 1980s and began to appreciate television as both an object of study and an object of fandom. When I began to teach television studies in the 1990s,

I would customarily refute claims that television was bad, being more interested in the actual operations of television institutions in society.

Then two things happened that (re-)kindled my interest in media resistance. I became dean of a diverse humanities faculty in the 2000s and experienced first-hand the deep ambivalence many in the humanities feel towards the media and media studies. There was still a sense that mass media objects were not worthy of academic attention, and that the discipline was slightly suspect, too celebratory and getting too much attention.

The second thing that happened was social media. After an initial warm welcome, online and social media began to provoke diverse expressions of resistance. In the 2010s, complaints began to pop up in conversations that reminded me of the anti-television stance of my childhood. As statements and confessionals about invasive media proliferated, the labels customarily used by media scholars and liberals to describe media resistance, of "media panic" and "technophobia" did not really seem to fit. In an era of ubiquitous media, it seems like we all need a measure of resistance, or at least a strategy for self-regulation, to keep our engagement with media in check.

And so the tables keep turning. I have written this book because I am curious about those who resist, and how media resistance is sustained as a powerful presence in our culture. I have also written it because I believe that media studies should devote more attention to expressions and acts of resistance, how they connect, persist and change.

The Book

New media divide opinion; many are fascinated while others are disgusted. This book is about those who dislike, protest and abstain from media – both new and old. The aim is to explore media resistance across media and historical periods, explain continuities and differences, and discuss how media resistance is sustained. The discussion is based on two questions asked in each chapter: What is at stake and what to do – how does media resistance inspire organized action?

Many current and historical works refer to media resistance. Books on digital media discuss the arguments of both enthusiasts and sceptics (see, for example, Bauerlein 2011; Creeber and Martin 2009; Baym 2010). Media and cultural historians describe "media panics" (Drotner 1999) and protests against controversial genres (see, for example, Nicholas' and O'Malley's 2013; Rowbotham and Stevenson 2003; Ferguson 2013).

Policy and censorship studies describe campaigns to restrict and limit media (see, for example, Heins 1993, 2007; Barker 1984a; Black 1994; Grieveson 2004). Studies of adaption and use describe and characterize the motivations of non-users and slow adopters (see, for example, Carey and Elton 2010; Helsper and Reisdorf 2013; Wyatt 2003).

Yet, despite the interest in media scepticism and dislike, few address media resistance as a more general phenomenon transcending types of media, historical periods and national borders. Few have also studied resistance as a common form of media reception: investigating motives, sources of inspiration and forms of action. As media becomes ubiquitous, more studies of voluntary abstention emerge, such as Krcmar's (2009) study of non-television families, Portwood-Stacer (2012) on Facebook rejectors and Woodstock (2014) on media resistance. There is also a relevant strand of studies focusing on resistance to new technology (see, for example, Bauer 1995a; Wyatt 2003). But media resistance has a long and complex history that deserves more intellectual scrutiny.

This book explores resistance from the early phase of mass media to present-day digital media. A retrospective perspective is particularly interesting nowadays, as new debates over digital media illuminate qualities of previous debates. Media history is not written once for all; new modes require new historical scrutiny and may change the way we understand the past. As today's media users struggle with aspects they are uncomfortable with – whether it is invasiveness, surveillance, content perceived to be problematic, or other features – a new look at the history of media resistance is fruitful in order to discuss what is recurring and what is changing over time.

Drawing on cases and examples from both sides of the Atlantic, media resistance is discussed as a diverse phenomenon encompassing political, professional, networked and individual arguments and actions. Based on sources such as political documents, press clippings, websites, organizational documents, non-fiction bestsellers and personal testimonies, the book explores narratives of resistance and how media is placed in a villainous and destructive role. The analysis also draws on dystopic fiction and film to show how themes in media resistance are depicted in popular culture. While resistance to media has inspired writers and film-makers, resisters have in turn been inspired by dystopic depictions. As will be noted throughout the book, media resistance does not depend on specific, detailed or even empirical evidence, whereas dystopic fiction remains a recurring source of inspiration.

Moralists, Luddites and Laggards

The study of media resistance cuts across fields and disciplines: cultural studies, sociology, media policy, and audience and technology studies. Although the approaches vary, there is a tendency to conceptualize resistance to media in rather negative terms: resistance is seen as a form of panic, an irrational reaction, caused by technophobia, fear, hysteria or social marginalization. The underlying premise is often that those who resist are moralists (subject to irrational moral "panics"), Luddites (against technology and progress), laggards (marginalized, slow adopters) or cultural pessimists (sceptical of popular culture and modern life).

Historically, much protest against the media has been grounded in moral judgements, and churches and moral movements have favoured censorship and restrictions (Ch. 2). In this sense, it is no surprise that media resistance is linked with moralism. However, those who study and discuss moral reactions often go further; characterizing campaigns and protests as "moral panics." Marshall McLuhan used the term "moral panic" as early as 1964 to describe the reactions of many "highly literate people" to the new "electric" media (McLuhan 1968, 91). British sociologist Stanley Cohen (1973) made the term widely known in his studies of reactions against youth behaviour in the 1960s. Since then, "moral panic" has been used to describe a wide variety of social protests, including protests against popular culture and new media. The concept is not just used in academia, but flourishes in journalism and public debate where it is used to describe a diverse set of reactions (see Barker 2013; Rowbotham and Stevenson 2003; Nicholas and O'Malley 2013; for overviews). Criticism of "moral panic" is also used by media operators as self-defence, indicating that critics are merely moralists and there is no need to take notice.

Academically, the tradition of "moral panic" deals with "mobilised and orchestrated scares," how fears are promoted to prepare the ground for political and legal interventions (Barker 2013, xv). The media have often contributed to public fears: Williams (2013) observes that the British press in the eighteenth century "heightened fear, anxiety and threats" (29), while McRobbie (1994) argues that increased competition in the late twentieth century made it "a standard journalistic practice to construct moral panics in the media" (198). Also the parallel concept of media panic deals with orchestrated scares, in this case, scares about the negative effects of new media. In media panics, media are "both instigator and purveyor of the discussion" (Drotner 1999, 596, see also Biltereyst 2004; McRobbie 1994).

Although the tradition focuses on orchestrated fears, there is a tendency that the labels of "panic," "hysteria" and "fear" rub off on those who protest. For example, in an article comparing social fears surrounding popular literature and Internet, Sutter (2003, 162) poses a typical dichotomy between the rational and hysterical:

> A balanced, cautious approach to new technologies and the uses to which they may be put, is of course sensible. However, not all critics of new media throughout history have been rational and balanced in their judgement. Both the arrival of cheap weekly publications in the Victorian era and the internet at the end of the twentieth century were subject to much hysteria, emphasising their supposed negative social effects, even blaming them for a range of social ills.

The distinction between the rational and the emotional/hysterical often appears in literature and public debate without much discussion. For example, Majorie Heins (1993), who has written extensively on media censorship, attributes popular protests and interventions to "emotions so powerful that they may interfere with rational thought" (2). Ironically, the idea that the masses were hysterical legitimated early media censorship; for example, there were concern for the allegedly "panicky" crowd drawn to early cinema (Grieveson 2004, 12). In recent times, those who want to restrict media are the ones seen as panicky moralists. Whether used about cinemagoers in the early 1900s or todays' media resisters, I would question whether the panic-label is adequate and suitable; it is always risky to place one position in the rational corner while hypothesizing that the other is irrational.

In this book, the concern for morality is discussed as only one of several motivations behind media resistance; just as important are concerns for culture, enlightenment, democracy, community and health. Concern for these values has led to reactions not just against content, but also against media technology and the media's functions in society. In this, as in other fields, those who resist new technologies are often conceptualized as Luddites; which has become shorthand for being anti-modernity and prone to simplistic technological determinism. The Luddites were British textile workers breaking mechanized looms in the early phase of the industrial revolution, and although their protest was more complex, the label is used generously to characterize any resistance to change (see, for example, Randall 1995). As the author Jonathan Franzen (2013) comments after having been called a Luddite for criticizing twitter:

> Not only am I not a Luddite. I'm not even sure the original Luddites were Luddites. (It simply seemed practical to them to smash the steam-powered looms that were putting them out of work).

Also resistance to communication technology tends to be explained in psychological terms. Bauer (1995b) shows how a confined body of literature in the 1980s and 1990s "employs 'anxiety' and 'phobia' as core concepts for understanding resistance to computers at school, at work and at home" (97). Resistance is seen "as a structural and personal deficit," it is "irrational, morally bad, or at best, understandable but futile" (Bauer 1995a, 2, see also Selwyn 2003, 103).

I will show examples of positions that both fit and do not fit the popular image of a Luddite, but will not attempt to determine whether protesters really are Luddites. Instead, the discussion will show how accusations of Luddism influence the way writers and activists frame their arguments and how they try to distance themselves from assumptions that they are simplistic and anti-technology. While it is of course, legitimate to discuss whether an argument is technologically determinist or anti-technology, this might not be the most interesting aspect of a text expressing media resistance. In this book, I attempt instead to understand such texts as sense-making efforts, drawing on an eclectic mix of perspectives and ideas in order to warn about, or explain, potential damage resulting from media's presence.

The label of "laggard" is also used about those who resist the media (see Selwyn 2003, 105). The theoretical definition of laggards comes from diffusion theory and the classical work *Diffusion of innovation* from 1962 (1995), which divides adopters into five ideal types (263–266). While the first three: innovators, early adopters and early majority, are described in positive terms, the two last: late majority and laggards, are described in negative terms. Laggards are described as backward looking:

> Laggards are the last in a social system to adopt an innovation. They possess almost no opinion leadership.... The point of reference for the laggard is the past.... Laggards tend to be suspicious of innovations and of change agents (265).

Rogers acknowledge that resistance may be "entirely rational" from the laggards' viewpoint, but that is because they are marginalized, or, as he puts it: "their resources are limited" (265). The tradition leaves little room for those who do not want to connect; as Selwyn (2003, 101) points out, questions regarding those who do not voluntarily use technology have "remained on the periphery of academic work on technology and society." With intensified emphasis on closing the digital gap, those who do not hook up are predominantly studied in order to identify barriers that can be overcome. Yet non-use cannot just be explained with reference to economic or social marginalization, non-users also report a lack of interest and a positive will not to connect (Reisdorf 2011, 408, see also; Helsper and Reisdorf 2013, 95). As media scholars, why someone is "not interested" in online communication should excite our intellectual curiosity, and it is important to examine motivations and arguments with an open mind rather than a pre-determined political goal.

Doomsday Prophets and Cultural Pessimists

Mass media are often awarded a central place in doomsday scenarios that "substitutes a catastrophic or a cyclic view of history for a progressive one" (Brantlinger 1983, 51). There are predictions of doom in many media-critical works, ranging from early condemnations of popular literature, to critique of the culture industry in the 1930s and 1940s, to anti-television-manifestos, and fictional portrayals of risks and dangers of media engagement. Those who resist media often use strong language and apocalyptic metaphors; hyperbolic discourses reinforce the impression of impending doom. In the book I refer to a range of predictions of bad media having bad consequences, and show how such predictions may travel across genres and historical periods. However, the point is not to evaluate the predictions or criticize them for being exaggerated or wrong, but rather to discuss media doomsday predictions as an integrated, often entertaining and inspirational element of culture itself.

An important point in the book is that one has to look beyond actions and arguments to understand how media resistance is sustained in our culture; the prevalence of resistant sentiments in society implies that themes in media resistance also pop up in works of art. Media resistance can be seen as a cultural resource, inspiring, among other things, entertaining (and scary) plots and storylines in dystopic fiction and film. From the all-out apocalypse described in *Brave new world*

(1932), *Nineteen Eighty-Four* (1949) and *Fahrenheit 451* (1953) (see Ch. 3), to the more limited doomsday scenarios in films such as *Being there* (1979), *Videodrome* (1983), *The Truman Show* (1989), *Disconnect* (2013) and *Her* (2014) (see Ch. 6), works of dystopian fiction and film provide speculative and fascinating answers to the question: What will happen if media continue to evolve along paths perceived to be destructive. In the same way as fictional accounts draw on real debates, participants in such debates, who express media resistance and scepticism, may be inspired by works of fiction. Indeed, another reason why this book include analysis of fictional sources is that many works of resistance refer more liberally to fictional predictions than to (empirical) media research (see Ch. 7).

While Brantlinger (1983, 37) argues "[d]oomsdaying, present to a greater or lesser extent in all ages, has become the chief mode of modern culture," Solomon and Higgins (1996, 236) see doomsday scenarios as particularly prevalent in American thought. In terms of media resistance, there are comparatively more pronounced predictions of doom in the US compared with Europe, and much of the material in this book comes from the US. However, this may also be due to the much stronger position of commercial media in the US, particularly commercial broadcasting. As critics often point out, the US was founded by believers in the Enlightenment who struggled for freedom of expression, but disappointment set in as media were seen to betray their mandate (Pierce 2010; Postman 2005a; Gore 2007). In contrast, European cultures draw on not only Enlightenment ideals but also come from a history of religious censorship and absolutist monarchy, their modern media traditions more influenced by Victorian ideas of "uplift" (Rowbotham and Stevenson 2003; Scannel and Cardiff 1991). Both in Britain and the Nordic countries there is a strong tradition of public service broadcasting, which have acted as a normative influence to a much larger degree than the public broadcasting service in the US (Croteau and Hoynes 2012, 81). In Scandinavia, media have to some extent been seen as part of the welfare state project; epitomized in terms such as "the media welfare state" (Syvertsen et al. 2014).

Instead of studying media resistance as moral or media panic, Luddism, lagging or cultural pessimism, this book sees media resistance as rooted in deep-seated values, from which the media are seen as destructive and counter-productive. A reaction against the media is always a reaction in favour of something else – something considered more important, tangible and valuable. Media resistance is a way of connecting the dots about what goes wrong in society; a form of theorizing or paradigm-construction that generates narratives of warning and explanation. In the book, I point out how resistance is grounded in the same broadly shared values as acceptance and celebration of media, and how the impression that such values are threatened or lost, resonate with writers and activists from different eras.

To say that media resistance is grounded in values is not to say that all is rational in media resistance, there is definitely a place for emotions here as in other historical and social theorizing (Rosenwein 2002; Williams 2013). But as emotions go, fear, hysteria and panic are not the only sentiments, and not the most common. Williams (2013) argues that media scholars have looked at different emotions, "[b]ut the predominant emotion that has taken up by the discipline has been fear" (29). In the material examined, a wider range of emotions emerges, including bewilderment, ambiguity, apprehension, cynicism, sadness and resignation. Perhaps the most prevalent emotions expressed in the texts are disbelief, distrust and disappointment; disbelief at what the media can do and portray, distrust in the media for not being a force of good, and disappointment when high hopes are thwarted. I also identify a high degree of reflexivity and self-reflexivity; at least in the later decades, sceptics and protesters are aware of the labels used to describe them and reflect on how these labels make it more difficult to develop a critical stance.

Media Resistance

The term "media resistance" is used as a broad term to discuss a range of negative actions and attitudes towards media. The Oxford English Dictionary defines resistance as "the refusal to accept or comply with something," and media resistance describes a refusal to accept the way media operate and evolve. Although resistance and criticism go hand in hand, media resistance implies more than a critique of the media; it is an argument linking the existence and functions of media in society with social ills and social change to the worse, and as such an imperative for change. Although media resistance may be triggered by specific media items (see, for example, Phillips 2008 on controversial films), the emphasis is on generalized forms of resistance; statements and protests against entire media or communication technologies, genres, platforms, systems or functions.

Writers and protesters may well be discussed in this book without self-identifying as media resisters; indeed the purpose is not to draw a firm line between resisters and non-resisters. Themes in media resistance overlap with themes in general media debates, and my point is to discuss media resistance in a broad rather than narrow sense. The term "resistance" is used because it alludes to more neutral research traditions than those equalling resistance with moralism, panic or Luddism (above). For example, Wyatt et al. (2002) use the term "resisters" to describe people who do not use a certain technology because they do not want to, and "rejectors" to describe those who have stopped using it because they find it inadequate. These two categories are separated again from the "excluded" and the "expelled" (Wyatt et al. 2002, 36). In a study of people who do not use *Facebook*, Portwood-Stacer (2012) distinguishes between passive and active forms of rejection and labels the active forms "refusal" – alluding to a broader cultural struggle (6). Woodstock (2014, 1983) uses the term "media resistance" to describe informants "who intentionally and significantly limit their media use," without necessarily implying that these are part of a wider cultural movement. I use the term "resisters," but also terms such as "sceptics," "protesters," "abstainers" and also "critics" indicating that there is a porous border between different forms of resistance and scepticism, as well as between discourses and activism.

In this book, I am less interested in fierce reactions and fundamentalism, and more interested in media resistance as an everyday phenomenon. In media history, there are plenty of incidents of media destruction, from sixteenth century book burning to the Taliban's destruction of TV-sets in Afghanistan. There are also societies such as the Amish, who "remain resolute in their refusal to tap certain technologies," including television (Kraybill 1994, 49). In the last centuries, physical destruction of media has been rare in the West, although there have been symbolic protests, such as the burning of 44 sets in 1975 in San Francisco in order to give spectators a "cathartic explosion" and "be free at last from the addiction to television" (cited from Winn 1980, 28). Ferguson et al. (2008, 311) describe an incident where protesters pulled game consoles out of arcades and set them on fire. Although such incidents are rare, they remain part of media resistance symbolism and folklore, and destruction and obliteration of various forms of media products also surface in dystopic fiction and film.

Resistance to cultural expressions and modes of communication can be dated back to the ancients, and most forms of communication have been subject to negative reactions (Fang 2015; Brantlinger 1983). In this book, the emphasis is on three phases that are particularly important for the understanding of resistance today: Resistance to media at the point of breakthrough for modern mass media in the nineteenth and early twentieth century (print, mass literature, cinema, radio, comics) (Ch. 2); resistance to television in the second half of the twentieth century (Ch. 4); and resistance to online and social media from around 2000 (Ch. 5). But the book not only discusses media in actual historical phases, it also deals with resistance in different phases of a medium's life: In Chapter 2, I discuss reactions to new media, in Chapter 4, resistance to television as a mature medium, and in Chapter 5, how resistance to online and social media evolved with new genres and services. Finally, the book deals with speculation and fantasies about all the bad things that can happen in a media-saturated society. Chapters 3 and 6 discuss dystopic fiction and films that portray the media as dangerous and destructive in different societies and eras, including the distant future.

The book does not attempt to define neither "media," nor "new media" precisely. Instead, the aim is to identify what types of media elements that provoke reactions and resistance, and how various forms of communication are lumped together by critics and sceptics. The book reflects the move from distinct media products and services, to electronic flow-media and developments towards convergence and ubiquity where "[a] clear-cut dichotomy no longer exists" between person-to-person and mass media (Carey and Elton 2010, 1). In the final phase, protesters and abstainers struggle to distinguish between useful and detestable aspects of increasingly converging media.

What is at Stake?

For each of the periods discussed in the book, I ask two questions. The first question is: What is at stake? Or more specifically: What are the underlying values and concerns that motivate resistance and scepticism?

The preoccupations in media resistance are not some peripheral concerns, but rather central narratives familiar from other political, cultural and social struggles. Based on a discussion of early mass media resistance in Chapter 2, I identify six concerns that are recurring for the different media discussed: Morality, culture, enlightenment, democracy, community and health. In the remaining chapters, I discuss how these values are interpreted in relation to later media and point to continuity and change.

The concerns for *morality* are grounded in the belief that media and cultural expressions should guide individuals in how to live a virtuous life (Brantlinger 1983). Resistance is based on claims that media do not fulfil this purpose and instead undermine moral values. The concern for *culture* is similarly based on the idea that media should aspire to raise cultural standards, but that print and electronic media rather produce cultures of mediocrity (Ward 1989, 79).

The third concern is for *enlightenment*. Enlightenment philosophers fought archaic political and economic structures, resisted dogma and superstition, and believed in each individual's ability to rise to a higher level (Solomon and Higgins 1996, 198–199). Resistance is grounded in criticism that media fail in its role as a public educator, and indeed may undermine educational efforts more generally; instead stimulating escapism, silliness and distraction. The call for liberty of the press was a vital aspect of the democratic revolution and a free press was considered a critical ingredient of politics (Keane 1991, 26–27). But instead of promoting truth, the media has been seen to undermine *democracy* through indoctrination, propaganda and "the manufacture of consent" (Lippman 1922).

The fifth concern is for *community*. Media and communication technology is often depicted as bringing people together, but to those who resist, media brings isolation (Fang 2015, 4). Resistance is linked with notions of mass society and the concern that industrialization, urbanization and mass media have undermined the communal basis of society (Dewey 1991). Finally, there is the concern for *health*. Resistance has been grounded in concern that media would destroy physical as well as mental health, leading to anything from "psychic infections" (Grieveson 2004, 12) to changes in brain structure, impoverished eyesight, addiction, obesity and many other ills.

In this book, I draw on a wide range of material to discuss how the concerns of media resistance are expressed and alluded to across genres, types of media, historical periods and national borders. I also pay particular attention to the evolvement of rhetoric and metaphors used to describe bad media – from "penny dreadfuls," via "the idiot box," to "The Internet is today's toilet wall" (see summary in Ch. 7).

What to Do?

The second question discussed in each chapter is this: What to do – what kind of action do statements of media resistance point to in order to remedy the problems identified, and what methods are used by activists, networks and individuals to deal with problematic media? In the chapters about dystopian literature and film, I have tweaked the question a little, asking instead to what degree the fictional works depict successful paths of action for characters, and where hope lies, if there is any, in the novels and films.

Media resistance is directed at many different entities: industry, legislators, content, genres, technologies, effects, users. Actions of resistance and protest can be classified along a continuum, from the political and legal protests to individual actions. In this book, I discuss political campaigning, aiming, usually, at prohibition, censorship or other forms for legal action. Furthermore, I discuss professional and institutional reactions; pointing to how educational, medical and religious professionals have endorsed media-resistance activities, and how these professions have been joined by writers, journalists and "techies" feeling overpowered by digital media in the last phase. The third type is networked resistance; I discuss organizations and networks that have provided platforms for and supported resistance activities. Finally, I discuss actions performed by or directed at individuals and families, from efforts to convince parents to restrict the use of media among the young, to more recent examples of media abstention, fasting and detox.

In the book I distinguish between arguments that the media are bad, but "tameable," and arguments that certain media, genres or technologies are irredeemable. To some extent, this parallels a distinction between resistance to content and resistance to the media's functions, which again parallels a distinction in media studies between studies of media effects and so-called medium theory. The latter tradition attributes more meaning to the mode of communications than to content (Meyrowitz 1985, 16; Croteau and Hoynes 2012, 299, see also Ch. 4). However, while such distinctions are easily made on the level of discourse, they are less useful in terms of distinguishing between different types of activism, as those who take action against or voice strong opposition to media, tend to dislike them for many different reasons.

Whether a medium, technology or genre is seen to be irredeemable or tameable also depends on the context; what is considered possible in a certain political climate. Over the last century, the context of media – and also media resistance – has changed drastically. In the nineteenth and early twentieth centuries protesters appealed to legislators for restrictions, censorship and even prohibition of some media and genres. Although political campaigning continues, in later decades, liberalization and convergence have made it more difficult to identify clear political goals. In the book,

I explore the transition from a political and legal orientation towards more personal media regulation, where self-help guides and websites inspire media detox and abstention.

Although this book draws on examples and cases from several countries, most notably the US, but also Britain and Scandinavia; the intention is not to do stringent comparative analysis. The purpose is instead to use examples and cases to show that media resistance is both situated and travels across borders. Books are translated, movements in one context align with movements in another, writers and campaigners are invited to speak at conferences and events; yet resistance also reflects historical and cultural specificities in different eras and contexts.

Open Access   This chapter is licensed under the terms of the Creative Commons Attribution 4.0 International License (http://creativecommons.org/licenses/by/4.0/), which permits use, sharing, adaptation, distribution and reproduction in any medium or format, as long as you give appropriate credit to the original author(s) and the source, provide a link to the Creative Commons license and indicate if changes were made.

The images or other third party material in this chapter are included in the book's Creative Commons license, unless indicated otherwise in a credit line to the material. If material is not included in the book's Creative Commons license and your intended use is not permitted by statutory regulation or exceeds the permitted use, you will need to obtain permission directly from the copyright holder.

CHAPTER 2

Resistance to Early Mass Media

Abstract Media resistance was shaped by industrialization and urbanization, and the debates over mass society and mass culture. The chapter reviews resistance to early mass media: print and books, serial fiction, cinema, radio and comics, and show how these media were seen to undermine morality, culture, enlightenment, democracy, community and health. The chapter discusses campaigns and protests against early mass media and shows that a common feature was a struggle for political and institutional control, prohibition or censorship.

Keywords Media history · Mass culture · Mass society · Censorship

SMASH THE VITASCOPE!

The first US exhibition of Thomas Edison's Vitascope, a Motion Picture projector, took place in 1896. Literary editor Herbert Stone protested:

> I want to smash the Vitascope. The name of the thing is itself a horror. Its manifestations are worse (cited from French and Petley 2007, 8).

Throughout history there have been many strong exclamations as to what people would like to do to media, although calls for destruction

---

*is used throughout the book to indicate my translation.

© The Author(s) 2017
T. Syvertsen, *Media Resistance*,
DOI 10.1007/978-3-319-46499-2_2

waned as mass media proliferated. This chapter explores media resistance and scepticism in the early mass media era, showing how historical conditions from the beginning shaped both media and concerns about their negative impact. I begin with resistance to writing, print and books, before moving on to the mass media emerging in the wake of the industrial revolution: serial literature, cinema, radio and comics.

Resistance is directed at both new and old media, but in this chapter, the emphasis is on resistance when the media were new. The early phases of a medium's life fascinate scholars as well as history buffs; this is the era when fantasy and speculation contribute to how a new medium is understood (Natale and Balbi 2014, 208, see also Marvin 1988; Boddy 2004). New media are met with high expectations, but also with ambiguity, distrust and dystopic visions. In the early phase of a medium's life, warnings are issued about potentially destructive effects; in later phases these may be overtaken by explanatory narratives where social ills are explained by reference to ongoing media influence.

The historical sweep in this chapter cannot do justice to the twists and turns of each medium's early history, the purpose is instead to identify what was at stake for resisters: What were the social and political projects that were perceived to be most profoundly challenged by emerging media? I show how concerns for morality and culture were complemented with concerns for enlightenment, democracy and community, and how the media were often considered a threat to mental and physical health. In addition to perspectives and arguments, the chapter discusses actors and actions; what were the methods proposed and employed to limit, curtail and restrict? Important sites of struggle in this early phase were the legal and political domains, but also schools, libraries, churches, public areas and homes. Examples and cases are drawn from the UK, the US and Scandinavia, with scattered examples from elsewhere, but the purpose is not to do a stringent comparative analysis. Instead, the aim is to identify concerns and actions that became emblematic and representative in a Western context, and had impact across national and social boundaries.

In the chapter, I am indebted to existing media and cultural histories, as well as historically informed discussions of media theory (see, for example, Bastiansen and Dahl, 2003; Brantlinger 1983; Scannell 2007, Ytreberg 2008, Storey 2009; Fang 2015). In addition, the chapter draws on expressions of protest, criticism and scepticism in articles, books, political documents and other non-fiction material.

Writing, Print, Books: Early Expressions of Resistance

Writers and commentators often date criticism of "new media" back to the ancients. According to Plato, Socrates opposed the teaching of writing. He disliked that text was mute and did not engage in dialogue, and warned that the alphabet and writing would create forgetfulness since people would no longer depend on memory (Plato around 370 BC, see also Fang 2015, 21). The position of Plato himself is also often cited; he advocated artistic censorship, believing that art should inspire "appropriate social attitudes and behaviour" (Solomon and Higgins 1996, 54). From the beginning of philosophy, a key question has been how to live a virtuous life, and moral philosophy, as well as various religious denominations, has prescribed rules of good behaviour (Solomon and Higgins 1996; Brantlinger 1983). Perhaps the strongest argument against new media has been that they have not supported this moral endeavour, but instead embody characteristics that threaten to undermine what is virtuous and valuable.

It is always risky to take a contemporary phenomenon and draw historical lines back to a time when conditions were entirely different. In this book, the emphasis is on media developing from the nineteenth century, and I make no claims to present a full history of media resistance. However, some historical observations are interesting in a *longue durée* perspective – a perspective that emphasizes continuities in structures and mentalities (Braudel 1980). Particularly interesting are early reactions to writing, print and books.

The shift from oral to written culture in ancient history is the first of many shifts in media modes and functions. In the early modern period, the invention of printing as well as the arrival of paper in Europe prompted a new shift in communicative modes. Printed material became important for trade, the rise in colloquial speech and the spread of dissenting ideas (Barnouw 1966, 3). But printed material also challenged the King and the Church, and undermined the religious monopoly on knowledge. The Church's reaction to the invention of printing was dual; printed bibles made God's words accessible, but the technology of printing could also be used to distribute unauthorized material. Reactions were brutal: In the sixteenth century, the Catholic Church prohibited reading of heretical writings, offending books were consigned to public bonfires, and an Index was drawn up of prohibited books (Fang 2015, 46ff). In contrast, lists of "good" books became the basis for collections and later public libraries (Hertel 1986, 347–348).

The duality in the Churches' reactions were mirrored by others' in the early modern era. In the essay *What is Enlightenment*, Kant (1997) encouraged fellow citizens to trust their own reasoning, and believers in enlightenment and universal education held high hopes for the revolutionary technology of print. But as mass distribution of printed material flourished, concern intensified about popular taste in content, and new lines were drawn between art and non-art, and between acceptable and non-acceptable genres (Newcomb 2002, 8). Each new genre was met with ambivalence; for example, when the novel became popular in England the eighteenth century, it was at first considered a "vulgar phenomenon" (Williams 1958, 306). In contrast, poetry, drama and the verse epic were seen as the ultimate literary genres (Öhman 2002, 10).

The immersion of readers in novel plots intensified concerns about copycat behaviour, a recurring theme in the history of media resistance. Would readers be able to distinguish between literary depictions and real life, or would they copy the behaviour of literary characters? A much discussed novel, which exemplifies the concerns raised by popular reading, was Goethe's *The Sorrows of Young Werther [Die Leiden des jungen Werthers]*, a 1774 bestseller about a young man committing suicide when he is unable to marry the woman he loves. The novel had a huge impact and gave rise to intense discussion on the ethical problem of suicide and whether it was morally responsible to depict suicide in print. *The Gentleman's Magazine* for 1784 reported the unfortunate destiny of a Miss Glover who was found dead with a copy of "*Werther*" under the bed; the magazine blaming "the evil tendency of that pernicious work" (cited from Swales 1987, 94–95). In 1775 the Leipzig city council responded to a petition from the theological faculty and made it an offence, punishable by fine, to sell copies of the novel, remaining in force to 1825 (97).

The debates over early print media illuminate the use of metaphors in media scepticism and resistance; there is a rich tradition of rhetorical expressions characterizing media and use of media negatively and many predate the mass media era. Several are linked with disease; Krefting et al. (2014) show how the public sphere in the eighteenth century expanded despite warnings about "the writing epidemic"*. The Danish writer Ludwig Holberg was among the critics, he expressed strong concern for the contagious "writing diarrhoea"* that prevailed in his time and urged "charlatans" from all classes not to pick up the pen and let their thoughts out (9). In other words, the development of writing, reading and books was marked by enthusiasm, but also ambivalence, disillusionment and resistance.

Serial Fiction: Poisoning the Mind

The period from 1850 to 1920 is described as the "the great technical revolution"* (Bastiansen and Dahl 2003, ch. 3). Universal education systems greatly extended literacy, and inventions in production and distribution technologies – printing presses and railway networks – made printed material widely available. Shorter working days, lamps and electricity allowed reading for leisure. The rise in advertising enabled new forms of financial support for popular media; Hilmes (2007, 20) describes "an explosion in numbers, forms and types of media" in the US between 1890 and 1920. Media went from being organs published by and for the elite, to be directed at people in general.

This was a great epoch of media resistance. Intellectuals and professionals had to come to terms with spectacular new forms of mass communication: based on not only the printed words but also electromagnetism, sound and images (Marvin 1988). To sceptics, popular media blossomed "like weeds on a hot day" (Hilmes 2007, 20).

The first genuinely popular genre was serialized fiction, emerging first in newspapers from the 1830. The stories drew inspiration from folk tales and oral culture; thrillers and mysteries, romance and historical epics, science fiction and horror could be found in the cheap volumes (Öhman 2002; Sutter 2003). Stories were sold for a dime in the US and a penny in the UK – hence the terms "Dime novel" and the more deprecating "Penny dreadful." Cheap literature was also called "pulp fiction" because of the rough pulp paper. Serial fiction was from the beginning considered an outright threat to culture: it was formulaic, with no literary merit, poor writing style, plot and characterization (Bierbaum 1994, 95). The voluminous character of the series – often several thousand pages – was attributed to the fact that authors received payments per sheet and were writing purely for money (Öhman 2002, 9). Since characters were to survive through a drawn-out narrative, the stories depended heavily on stereotypes. Ethnic stereotypes in popular fiction came "complete with predictable occupations and phonetically rendered dialects" (Bierbaum 1994, 95).

Popular fiction drew condemnations on moral grounds. The moral criticism continued to be based in the belief that literature should depict good behaviour and elevate individuals to a higher moral level (Drotner 1999, 603). In popular fiction, heroes were often lawless, such as pirates and highwaymen. Female characters were active and strong-willed, and sometimes lawless too, and it was commonplace to warn that popular literature would teach young people criminal behaviour (Sutter 2003, 166). The new genres were seen as particularly detrimental to the young, but women and working class men were also seen to be vulnerable to their influence (Öhman 2002, 12). Publishers were prosecuted; an extract from a criminal indictment for obscene libel in Britain stated that the defendant intended to "debauch, poison and infect the minds" of youth (cited from Lewis 2003, 145). Health threats were imminent; a US official report from 1876 referred to warnings from physicians that reading romantic literature would lead to disorders of the "nerve centres," which had "so alarmingly increased" (cited from Bierbaum 1994, 93).

The resistance against popular fiction also reflected concern for enlightenment and popular education. Efforts to teach the population to read were motivated by a desire to advance learning and maturity, whereas serial fiction was seen to encourage passive reading, romantic fantasizing and escapism. If people wanted to read, they should read something useful: geography, history and statistics, argued Swedish editor C.F. Bergstedt in an 1851 essay about "wretched literature"*. Serialized fiction caused young men to have "no energy for serious and beneficial work"* and young women to sacrifice "happiness, peace of conscience and progress for frivolity and entertainment"* (cited from Öhman 2002, 11).

First among those who resisted popular literature were the religious and literary establishments, with some support from the medical profession. But also to the relatively newer professions of teachers and librarians, resistance became an integrated element of organizational and professional ideology. "[T]he whole idea of fiction in the library was one which the profession wrestled with for many years," writes Bierbaum of US librarians (1994, 100). Librarians as a rule strongly denounced serial literature, and kept it out through the means available: selection lists, catalogues, including "not to be circulated" lists (Bierbaum 1994, 94). In schools, the main strategy was to "suppress it, pretend it does not exist, and in this way express their contempt"*, writes Tvinnereim about the early attitudes of Norwegian teachers (1978, 81).

The metaphors used about popular literature were inspired by the problems of the day, metaphors alluding to disease, garbage and sanitation flourished. Popular literature was likened to poison and pollution, epidemics, infestation, sewage, garbage, rottenness and thrash (see Lewis 2003, 145; Sutter 2003, 165; Öhman 2002, 9; Fang 2015, 48). The first urban sewage systems date back to the same time as serialized fiction, around 1840, and whereas uncontrolled sewage poisoned the body, literature was seen to poison the mind.

Cinema: Education for Crime

Cinema shows began around 1900, and cinema rapidly became "the dominant institution in popular culture" (Black 1994, 6). Cinema transcended class, ethnic, gender and national differences, and soon became a controversial medium on both sides of the Atlantic. Movies were seen to rapidly intensify the process of demoralization; it drew young and vulnerable people out of their homes, tempted them into dark spaces and served them content of low quality and despicable moral standard (Grieveson 2004, 13, see also; Pearson 1984, 93; Drotner 1999, 605; Black 1994, 9). Young women were seen to be corrupted by movies romanticizing "illicit" love affairs and young men were incited to criminal behaviour by films "glorifying criminals" (Black 1994, 9). Instead of teaching the values and competences needed by the young and uneducated, they provided a different form of education; across national boundaries cinema was labelled "education for crime," "schools of vice and crime" (Black 1994, 10), a "training school of mischief, mockery, lawbreaking and crime" (Grieveson 2004, 15) and a "training ground for prostitution and robbery" (Thompson and Bordwell 2010, 29).

In response to the cinema's illusions of reality, new medical metaphors, involving psychiatry and mind control, became part of the vocabulary of resistance. Austrian psychiatrists Josef Breuer and Sigmund Freud had introduced hypnosis as a treatment for hysteria in the 1890s and hypnosis later became a metaphor for media effects. Cinema allegedly led to "surrender, under conditions of hypnotic receptivity, to the cheapest emotional appeals," wrote F. R. Leavis in 1930 (2006, 14). Compared to the cinema, popular fiction suddenly appeared more innocent, an argument spelled out by a Kansas philosophy professor:

> [P]ictures are more degrading than the dime novel because they represent real flesh and blood characters and import moral lessons directly through the senses. The dime novel cannot lead the boy further than his limited imagination will allow, but the motion picture forces upon his view things that are new, they give firsthand experience (cited from Black 1994, 10).

This is one of many statements where genres that were widely condemned, appear more respectable because new genres are seen to be worse. Compared with popular fiction, the cinema was also seen to expose users to more serious health risks; risks of fire in unsafe buildings with inflammable nitrate films, concern that spitting in theatres would spread disease, unease over whether flickering lights would damage eyesight and induce epilepsy (Pearson 1984, 95; French and Petley 2007, 7). Familiar metaphors were used to describe cinema, such as dirt, filth and trash, but also new diagnoses were hinted at with metaphors such as "nickel delirium" (Black 1994, 6).

From around 1910, state and industry censorship boards emerged locally and nationally. In the US, local censorship boards were formed from 1908, and the industry allowed films to be censored to achieve respectability (Thompson and Bordwell 2010, 29). In Europe, virtually every country established some form of censorship, in Norway from 1913. In the UK, an act of law from 1909 required local authorities to issue licences to safe cinemas, but soon authorities also interfered with content. By 1912 the British Board of film Censors was established, becoming the accepted self-governance board from 1913 (Robertson 1989, 1).

For those who resisted cinema's presence and potential influence, pushing for political and institutional control was an obvious choice. Books and print had been subject to censorship, and when cinema emerged in the early 1900s, the police already had both in Europe and the US authority to withdraw licences from music halls, variety shows and other public spectacles if performers included offensive material (Mathews 1994; Nymo 2002, 20).

The campaigns to censor cinema were coalitions, with some types of professions and social activists involved across national borders. Churches and clergy of different denominations organized protests and boycotts of films judged immoral by church authorities (Black 1994, 2). Churches were joined by social reform movements for juvenile protection, virtuous lifestyles and temperance. In the US, the Progressive reform movement fought corruption, child labour, unsafe houses and factories, prostitution and alcoholism, but also "immoral" media – from books and newspapers to cinema (Black 1994, 8). Nymo (2002, 22) points to the activism of teachers as instrumental to achieve Norwegian cinema censorship; the teachers' seminars and the enlightenment ethos laid the foundation for a professional self-confidence and status that teachers could draw on in their struggle to restrict popular culture.

Many women and women's groups were active campaigners (Evensmo 1992, 61; Black 1994, 9; Nymo 2002, ch. 2). Middle class ideals presumed that women were virtuous and should act as moral guardians, and female reformers became a counterpart to masculine pursuits such as drinking alcohol and using prostitutes (Grieveson 2004, 27, 29). Censorship is often seen as a class issue (Mathews 1994, 1), yet campaigns drew support from across the political spectrum, also from labour representatives who saw the movie industry as "capitalist" and "speculative" (Nymo 2002, 35).

Radio: Risk of Contagion

Early radio was blamed for a lot of things: "dizzy spells, changes in weather, creaky floorboards," Barnouw writes (1966, 103) and cites the example of a farmer complaining to a Louisville station that radio waves had killed a blackbird and potentially might kill him. In general, however, radio was met with the kind of enthusiasm that would later greet the Internet (Ch. 5); a discourse that "glorified radio's special properties" to unify disparate communities and build a national culture (Hilmes 1997, 1). But as radio became a mass medium, radio was subject to similar warnings and scepticism as other mass media, in particular concern that radio would undermine cultural standards, and be used as a tool to threaten democracy.

Radio was first used for ship-to-shore communication in the early 1900s, but was soon embraced by enthusiastic amateurs (Briggs 1985; Dahl 1975; Barnouw 1966). With the outbreak of World War I in 1914, amateur activity was suspended, and the initiative passed to the armed forces (Dahl 1975; Hilmes 2007; Briggs 1985). David Hendy, who has studied the development of wireless on the eve of World War I, describes an atmosphere of "control, paranoia and anxiety" (2013, 77). An important metaphor to describe the negative effect of radio was that of contagion; "the fear that wireless could spread information – or more precisely *mis*information – in an uncontrolled way." Wireless was invisible, synchronous, and messages could be heard by anybody. "It was increasingly clear that, given the special qualities of wireless, it needed to stay in the 'right' hands" (81).

But whose hands were right? After the war, controversy erupted in many countries over how radio should be controlled, involving state actors as well as social and cultural movements, manufacturers and advertisers, and educational institutions. The different paths taken had important implications for the development of broadcasting, and also for the evolvement of media resistance.

In the US, radio proliferated with a multitude of operators, many of which were universities and educational establishments. But "apathy," "disgust" and "weariness" set in (Barnouw 1966, 173) as interference led to "chaos." Proponents of educational and public service lost out as the 1927 Radio Act turned radio into a commercial medium run by networks, although more regulated than press and movies (Hilmes 2007, 44). In Europe, in contrast, private companies operating on a licence were replaced by state monopolies. The British Broadcasting Corporation (BBC) was established in 1927 in an atmosphere of "choice between monopoly and confusion" (Briggs 1985, 33); its mandate to provide national broadcasting with "no concessions to the vulgar" (55). In his *Broadcast over Britain*, the first Director-General of the BBC John Reith refused to accept that radio should give people "what they want." Few know what they want, and very few what they need, Reith proclaimed, and said that "our responsibility is to carry into the greatest possible number of homes everything that is best in every human department of knowledge, endeavour and achievement, and to avoid the things which are, or may be hurtful" (Reith 1924, 34).

In the US, where radio developed commercially, criticism erupted over moral standards. In a more profound way that other media, radio transcended boundaries of age, class, gender and geography, as well as between public and private spaces. The base in advertising was seen to draw radio towards "the vulgar, the barbaric and the illegitimate" (Hilmes 2007, 55). Of particular concern was jazz music, which, like many other forms of popular culture, was seen as "degrading" and "lowers all the moral standards"; according to protesters jazz left the listeners "incapable of distinguishing between good and evil, between right and wrong" (cited from Hilmes 1997, 48). In Europe, the BBC attempted to "root out" American influence and preserve a greater distance from the audience; the style was different from the friendly, informal and democratic style of American radio (Scannell and Cardiff 1991, 293). Yet, British radio was also criticized for undermining morality and culture. Wolfe (1984) notes that churches were sometimes positive, but "more often cautious and belligerently negative" to radio, believing it to "threaten clerical and ecclesial autonomy" (xxii, see also Brigg 1965, part II). British literary critic F. R. Leavis in 1930 expressed concern about passive listening and saw radio to have a standardizing influence that "hardly admits of doubt" (2006, 14).

Perhaps the strongest concern surrounding radio was that it could aid threats to democracy. During World War I, the media were used, for the first time, in a large-scale effort to control and manipulate public opinion (Ward 1989, 58). From the time the Nazi Government took power in

Germany in the 1930s, the threat became even more direct, as radio, film and public loudspeakers were used to rally support and mobilize the masses (113). Members of the Frankfurt school, who had sought refuge in the US to escape Nazi persecution in Germany, were dismayed by the use of media for propaganda. However, Horkheimer and Adorno saw no guarantee in the US commercial radio model:

> In America it collects no fees from the public, and so has acquired the illusory form of disinterested, unbiased authority which suits Fascism admirably. (1997, 159)

The debate over radio prompted new stark metaphors, such as "contagion," but also "chaos in the ether" and "the tower of babel" (e.g. Barnouw 1966). The biblical legend of the Tower of Babel – where different languages are God's punishment to Man – symbolized human curiosity and desire, but also arrogance leading to chaos and confusion. Radio was seen as having great potential for good, but in the war-torn first half of the twentieth century, it was also seen as a potential means of destruction.

COMICS: HORROR AND MUTILATIONS

The sale of comic books exploded in the late 1940s and early 1950s, during and in the direct aftermath of World War II. While many of the comics were innocent enough, with themes familiar from popular culture, others broke new ground in terms of sex, violence and horror. The resistance against comic books marks a shift to an era where traditional values confront a more liberal cultural climate (Gilbert 1986, 13–14). Comics were part of the wartime and post-war boom in popular culture, but the short distance to the atrocities of war also led to astonishment and disbelief as to the level of violence and brutality.

Again, the content was argued to be more amoral, and generally worse, than that of previous media. In addition to horror and violence; protest erupted over the portrayal of sexually active and powerful women, evil children, and what critics saw as role models for homosexuality (in Batman and Robin and Wonderwoman) (Wertham 2004; first publ. 1954, 190–192, 234, see also; Lepore 2014). Until the comic book era, alleged the influential US psychiatrist and anti-comics campaigner Frederic Wertham, "there were hardly any serious crimes such as murder by children under twelve" (2004, 155). Now, however, there were evidence of "a significant correlation between crime comics reading and the more serious forms of juvenile delinquency" (164).

Fredric Wertham was an important force in the anti-comics' campaign. From 1948, he wrote critical pieces in magazines such as *The Ladies Home Journal* and *Readers Digest* (Bastiansen and Dahl 2003, 344). *Seduction of the Innocent*, his 1954 book, had "enormous influence" both in the US and Europe (Barker 1984a, 56–57). Reibman (2004, xi) characterizes Wertham as "a traditional left-wing European intellectual and product of the Enlightenment tradition"; as a first generation Jewish immigrant from Germany in the 1920s he finds it ironic that Wertham should be characterized as a "reactionary." Yet, Wertham's ferocious critique of comic books is yet another illustration that resistance to media and genres have come both from left and right.

In later decades, Wertham has been criticized for both misrepresenting content (Barker 1984a) and fabricating evidence from clinical trials (Johnston 2013). Wertham himself, however, was frustrated that he did not get more support from science and academia. After a description of "Jungle comics" which "specialise in torture, bloodshed and lust in an exotic setting" he sighs:

> Whenever I see a book like this in the hands of a little seven-year-old boy, his eyes glued to the printed page, I feel like a fool to have to prove that this kind of thing is not good mental nourishment for children! What is wrong with the prevailing ethics of educators and psychologists that they have silently permitted this kind of thing year after year...? (31)

Wertham's comment reflects exasperation that experts were not unanimous; indeed, the debate about comics reflects disappointment over the early studies of media effects. In a 1954 Norwegian parliamentary debate about comics, there are references to Wertham's argument, but also to experts disputing the copycat effect (516). It is lamented that no unanimous scientific conclusions have been reached despite this being an issue which scientists wrestle with all over the world (1954, 509, 510, see also Lepore 2014). For some members of the Norwegian Parliament, however, the level of violence was indication enough that something had to be done. As one member, Erling Wikborg, argued (St.tid 1954, 508),

> Many of these series – and this is serious – undermines respect for human dignity. They often degrade women. Sometimes other races are degraded.

The series are filled with all dreadful possibilities in terms of brutality, torture, murder and many kinds of crimes. Some series even depicts crippled, deformed and coloured people as especially criminal.*

Great sacrifices had been made during the war to protect civilized life, democracy and enlightenment, and now comics laden with misogyny, Nazism, racism and negative stereotyping became popular entertainment.

Campaigns against comics erupted simultaneously in many countries and led to legislation or self-regulation (Bastiansen and Dahl 2003, 346). In the US, Wertham campaigned for a law against the sale of violent comics to children under fifteen, and public hearings and legal action followed (Gilbert 1986, 106). While a self-censorship Comics code was adopted in the US in 1954, "labelling the suitability of each comic book now published" (Reibman 2004, xxvii), so-called horror comics were outlawed in Britain in 1955 (Barker 1984a, 5).

Allies in the struggle against comics were teachers, scientists, librarians, psychologists, doctors and police. In Britain, the arguments against comic books resonated with religious, educational and political interests, including Communist Party members who were concerned about Americanization and the corruption of the young (Barker 1984a, 29). In a parallel to the campaign for cinema censorship (above), Barker points to the National Union of Teachers as a decisive force in the campaign against British horror comics (1984a, 15). The educational and literary professions were particularly incensed by the industry's attempt to achieve respectability for popular culture through the use of high culture. Already Shakespeare plays had been adopted for the cinema (Thompson and Bordwell 2010, 29–30) and now they were put into comic strips: "Shakespeare and the child are corrupted at the same time" is Wertham's verdict on the marketing of comic-book Macbeth with the slogan "a dark tragedy of jealousy, intrigue and violence adapted for easy and enjoyable reading" (143, see also MacDonald 2011).

Publishers claimed that comics were good for children, teaching them to read; trying to capitalize on the higher legitimacy of print compared with image-based media. But the protesters did not buy it. According to Wertham, comics prevented children from developing the necessary left-to-right eye movements (127), prompted the habit of gazing rather than reading (139), destroyed the taste for good books (140), made children bad spellers (144), and taught words which were not proper words, such as ARGHH, WHAM, THUNK, YEOW, BLAM (145).

Although some restrictions were initiated, campaigners were not content; there was a sense that the legal path was becoming more difficult to pursue, and support for censorship was vanishing. In Norway, Wikborg expressed disappointment that authorities did not recognize that comics were downright criminal (St.tid 1954, 518):

> If prosecutors would monitor these comics with greater attention, they would find more than one opportunity to use the provisions of the Criminal Code. I am thinking of para 140 of incitement to crime, para 142 about blasphemy, para 160 which speaks of public instruction in the use of explosives to commit crimes. We also have paragraphs 322 and 323 of criminal content in printed publications. We already have a number of provisions that can be used, but I have the impression that the prosecution has been rather hesitant when it comes to these issues.*

Wikborg, a lawyer as well as a parliamentary representative for the Christian People's Party would continue to oppose new media; four years later he would deem television to be "exceedingly dangerous"* (St.tid. 1957, 2458–2459) and he also believed the Norwegian radio corporation to have "skeletons in their closets"* (St.tid 1954, 509).

Reactions against comics stimulated new metaphors, which were both sexual and violent. Norwegian author Bjørn Rongen saw comics as "spiritual rape of minors"*, whereas a Danish author Tørk Haxthausen pigeonholed them as "education for terror"* in 1954 (Bastiansen and Dahl 2003, 345). Comics induced depravity and destroyed human souls, hence, the title of Wertham's book "Seduction of the Innocent" and metaphors used by him such as an "orgy of brutality" (111).

WHAT IS AT STAKE?

The preoccupations of media resistance are not some peripheral concerns; they are connected with broader cultural, social and political struggles at the time. As noted in the introduction, six recurring values have been identified in media resistance from the early mass media era; new media were seen to undermine morality, culture, enlightenment, democracy, community and health.

In the early phases of resistance the most prevalent values that the media were seen to undermine was morality and culture. Media and cultural depictions were conceived as vehicles to raise standards, both morally and in terms of taste and quality, and resistance reflected disappointment when these expectations were not met. The emergence of the first mass media coincided with the height of Victorian morality; the prominence of the British Empire ensured that Victorian values spread across the world and shaped the ideals of the new middle classes (Sundin and Willner 2007, 141; Black 1994, 21–22). Central to Victorian morality was that the upper classes should inspire and raise the standards of the lower class; Victorian authors produced stories of poor children and families following the path of virtue (Fang 2015, 75), whereas new media "delighted in ridiculing 'Victorian values'" (Black 1994, 7).

What critics saw as vulgarity and depravity intensified with each new medium, and so did also the conviction that culture was at stake. "It is commonplace today that culture is in crisis," stated British literary critic F. R. Leavis in the 1930 pamphlet *Mass Civilization and Minority Culture* (2006, 13). Leavis saw the emerging media as contributing to "a process of levelling-down" leading to passive consumption and loss of taste:

> Broadcasting, like the films, is in practice mainly a means of passive diversion... it tends to make active recreation, especially active use of the mind, more difficult (14).

Leavis represents a position where high culture and cultural aspirations are seen as the basis for civilized life. Culture represents man's best achievements and high morality, whereas the mass media represented low culture and amorality (Storey 2009). Although the perspective has lost ground, Storey considers the approach "foundational," still representing the "common sense" approach in some circles (33). From the left, the mass media were seen as agents of standardization and uniformity, destroying aristocratic high culture as well as authentic folk culture. Under the prevailing conditions, argued Horkheimer and Adorno (1997; first publ. 1944), "all mass culture is identical" (121) and "broadcast programs are all exactly the same" (122). Instead of contributing to enlightenment and social consciousness, popular media destroyed the masses by drowning them in pleasure (143).

Those who protest against media are often conceptualized as reactionary or backward; and much media resistance in the early phases hark back to a nostalgic past. But arguments and positions also point in other directions. On the one hand, there is criticism that media are destroying what is dear and valuable, on the other hand, there are arguments that the media stand in the way of progress. These latter arguments reflect not only disappointment that media depicted bad rather than good behaviour, but also disappointment that the emerging media did not, to a stronger degree lend themselves to progressive causes such as educational enlightenment and improvement of public health. Progressive campaigners on both sides of the Atlantic were disappointed with the escapist public, and media that prioritized triviality, superstition and frivolous entertainment. In the long run, it was argued, this would hamper the development of mature and competent citizens, and prevent youngster from developing into competent and healthy adults.

From the eighteenth century, authorities visibly increased their public health ambitions and a steep decline in mortality followed, but the industrial revolution brought new health risks, such as pollution and epidemics (Sundin and Willner 2007). Many saw the emerging media as part of the new risks, not only were there concern for eyesight, brain damage, mental distortion and "psychic infections" (cited from Grieveson 2004, 12), there were also concerns that spectators would burn to death or catch infections in dilapidated cinema theatres.

The debate over early mass media reflected the concerns over mass society; concepts such as "mass culture," "mass art," "mass entertainment" and "mass media" were all coined in the interwar period. The problem of the masses was a common theme in social thought, whether Marxist, Christian or liberal (Bastiansen and Dahl 2003, 237–238). On the one hand there was concern that the masses were inherently amoral and destructive, in the words of Spanish mass society theorist José Ortega y Gasset: "The mass crushes beneath it everything that is different, everything that is excellent, individual, qualified and select" (1993, first publ. 1930, 18). On the other, there were concern about authoritarian states indoctrinating the masses with the use of media propaganda, a concern reinforced by the rise of totalitarianism in Italy, Germany and the Soviet Union.

The concern with mass society is also relevant for the argument that mass media would undermine community. Media and communication technology is often depicted as bringing people together, but to sceptics and critics media brought isolation. As Fang puts it (2015, 4),

> For the many centuries during which most of the world was illiterate, people received their information from each other, from travelers and from their local priests. Entertainment came from one another in the form of singing, dancing and story-telling. The shared element was community. Each other. Media brought isolation.

According to mass society theorists, uniformity and conformity characterized modern societies, eroding traditional bonds and communal solidarity. In the US, the Progressive reform movement worked to reform urban America by returning to values of local communities (Geraghty 2009, 4). The philosopher John Dewey was a major progressive theorist, who shared the concern that industrial society and mass media were destroying the communal basis of society (Dewey 1991; first publ 1927; see also Hilmes 2007, 18). Dewey describes a situation where, in the 1920s, there were already too much media – the telegraph, telephone, radio, mail and printing press. He argued that "the physical and external means of collecting information...have far outrun the intellectual phase of inquiry and organization of the result" (1991, 180).

The six concerns – for morality, culture, enlightenment, democracy, community and health – are not mutually exclusive; they are linked and overlap, but also illustrate that media resistance may emerge from different, and often contradictory positions. In addition to concerns about different values, there were resistance to different aspect of the media: technology, structure, content and functions. Resistance evolves in response to each new medium and mode shift: From oral to written communication, from writing to print, from print to images, from oral to radio, from photographs to movies. It is interesting to observe how protesters often contrast the functions of a new medium with a medium already an object of resistance; while this may alert sceptics to new dangers, the effect would also have been to make existing media appear more innocent, thus aiding the process of media acceptance.

What to Do?

For resistance to be manifest it is not sufficient that someone is concerned; organizations, politicians, professionals or other actors must also act publicly, suggest measures and organize protest (Phillips 2008). But what could those who resisted new media really do? Herbert Stone wanted to "smash the Vitascope" and the Church in early modern Europe destined objectionable books to public bonfires. As we get closer to own time, suggestions that media be destroyed or banned become less frequent. In the early era of the mass media, in the nineteenth and twentieth centuries, protestors largely fought for legal, political and institutional control and censorship. Cinema was censored from around 1910; the outbreak of World War I led to state takeover of radio, in the 1920s radio became regulated as public companies in Europe, in the 1940s and 1950s anti-comics campaigners succeeded in instigating prohibition and censorship.

In order for censorship and control to function, professions and experts must exercise discretion and authority. Churches, schools and libraries were important gatekeepers for keeping out undesirable printed material. With popular literature, as well as movies and comics, panels of experts were set up to vet, evaluate and recommend. Educational, religious and medical professions were also influential in advisory bodies for early broadcasting. State and public broadcasting institutions, as well as the US radio networks and their self-regulatory mechanisms, are prominent examples of institutional control of media.

In the cases I have discussed from early mass media history, I have not seen material where consumers pledge abstinence because they were convinced that media were bad for them. But there are plenty of efforts to convince others to abstain from media. A whole range of social and political movements was active in the struggle against early popular media and genres. Campaigners used parents' meeting to mobilize support and urged parents to behave responsibly and restrict youngsters' media consumption. Appeals were directed at producers and distributors to behave responsibly. For example, in a 1954 parliamentary debate on comics in Norway, a representative suggested an information campaign to "get newsagents and tobacconists to refuse to sell this filth"* (St.tid 1954, 515).

Resistance travels across borders and protesters, such as Fredric Wertham, helped to inspire campaigns in many countries. There are also references to the involvement of international bodies, in the case of comics, critics refer to debates in UNESCO, a United Nations agency established in 1945 that would later develop a strong media-critical agenda (St.tid 1954, 507–508). Studies show that the methods used were similar from one campaign to the next (see for example Grieveson (2004) on the US and Nymo (2002) on the Norwegian cinema campaigns, and Barker (1984a) on the UK comics campaign). The campaigners' toolkit was similar to that of any social or political activist of the twentieth century: public meetings were held, petitions were directed at politicians, pamphlets produced, lists of speakers were offered to conferences, letters were written to the press, alliances built with experts and professional bodies. A method that was often used in this early period was to collect particularly despicable pieces of content to show to legal authorities, politicians, clergy and press in order to create a public outcry. Likewise, campaigners collected examples of stories indicating potential copycat behaviour. As one British anti-comic campaigner described the situation in retrospect,

> We looked – it is almost wicked to say this – with eager anticipation for a story in the press of a child who had done something so that we could point to the comics. And if one had done something, then this supported our case. And we called this research. (Joe Benjamin, anti-comics campaigner, cited in Barker 1984a, 182)

The quote illustrates how protesters did "research" and how many yearned for scientific evidence and proof of media's detrimental character. Systematic media research was of course initiated; such as the 1928 Payne Fund study on cinema effects and the Office of Radio Research with Paul Lazarsfeld and colleagues at Columbia University from the 1930s (Ytreberg 2008, 40). But as the period of early mass media resistance came to an end, there was reason to be disappointed, as expert evidence became increasingly contradictory. Those critical and sceptical of the way media transformed society would not get an unambiguous answer from science, but there were other sources of inspiration: not least engaging and popular fiction stories where bad media played a part in undermining civilization and leading to apocalypse.

Open Access This chapter is licensed under the terms of the Creative Commons Attribution 4.0 International License (http://creativecommons.org/licenses/by/4.0/), which permits use, sharing, adaptation, distribution and reproduction in any medium or format, as long as you give appropriate credit to the original author(s) and the source, provide a link to the Creative Commons license and indicate if changes were made.

The images or other third party material in this chapter are included in the book's Creative Commons license, unless indicated otherwise in a credit line to the material. If material is not included in the book's Creative Commons license and your intended use is not permitted by statutory regulation or exceeds the permitted use, you will need to obtain permission directly from the copyright

CHAPTER 3

Evil Media in Dystopian Fiction

Abstract Media resistance is a recurring theme in contemporary culture, and comprises familiar concerns that can be used to create speculative and readable stories and plots. The chapter discusses key works of dystopic fiction that have inspired media resistance until today: Huxley's *Brave New World* (1932), Orwell's *Nineteen Eighty-Four* (1949) and Bradbury's *Fahrenheit 451* (1953). All three novels portray authoritarian societies where the growth of mass media represents a danger to civilization. The screen media (cinema and television) are depicted as particularly bad, whereas print culture and books are depicted as representing hope for humanity.

Keywords Orwell · Huxley · Bradbury · Dystopic fiction · Media prophesies

DOOMSDAY WITH A CAPITAL D

In Edward Bellamy's futuristic novel *Looking Backward,* published in 1888, the protagonist finds himself in the year 2000, where new media entertain and enlighten citizens. The dominant medium in this utopian society is an advanced telephone, which brings music, sermons and lectures to every home (Bellamy 1996). In Bellamy's society, citizens prosper and the media strengthen culture, community and democracy. In contrast, there are plenty of utopian narratives – in fiction as well as feature films – where the media play a destructive and negative role.

In order to understand media resistance as a pervasive element in our culture, it is worthwhile to move beyond public debates and political campaigns and into the realm of fiction. The prevalence of resistant sentiments in society implies that themes in media resistance also pop up in works of art, and in this book, I specifically discuss dystopic fiction and films (see Ch. 6). Fiction can go further than non-fiction in predicting and imagining the future, and can wrap warnings about destructive media in readable and entertaining plots and storylines. As McNair points out in his analysis of films featuring media and journalists (2010, 19), fictional works contribute to "an ongoing public conversation" and may reinforce public concerns. Depictions of utopian societies, from Thomas Moore's *Utopia* in the sixteenth century and onwards, have served as frames of references in cultural and political debates, and have inspired policies and manifestos.

The three works selected for discussion in this chapter are among the most influential in the Western literary canon: Aldous Huxley's *Brave New World* (2006, first published 1932), George Orwell's *Nineteen Eighty-Four* (2008; first published 1949) and Ray Bradbury's *Fahrenheit 451* (2013; first published 1953). The novels, of which the first two are English and the third American, have fascinated countless readers, are translated into many languages, and have been adapted into movies, TV-films, comic books, stage plays and reality shows. Their authors continue to appear on rankings of the most influential English writers of the twentieth century (e.g., the novels occupy first, second and third place on the online list *Best dystopian Science fiction books*, 2015, see also Baccolini and Moylan 2003, 1). The novels have been praised for their predictions of major upheavals, from the Nazi and Soviet atrocities, to the post-war consumer boom, to recent incidents of terrorism and surveillance. Often the novels, and especially *Nineteen Eighty-Four* and *Brave New World*, are contrasted as representing a "soft" vs. "hard" version of dystopia (see, for example, Atwood 2007; Postman 2005a). Yet all three depict the destruction of civilization, as we know it – these are doomsday narratives with a capital D.

Furthermore, all three novels portray apocalypses where media and communication technology play a decisive role. As such, they are excellent illustrations of the point that media resistance is a cultural resource, providing writers and directors with themes and plots recognizable across the globe. And in the same way as fictional accounts may draw on real debates, participants in such debates may draw on dystopic fiction. In addition to their canonical status, these novels, and in particular Orwell's and Huxley's, are discussed here because they have served as specific sources of inspiration in media resistance. As pointed out in the introduction, there are predictions of doom in many media-critical works, and many such works are littered with references to these particular novels (Chs. 4–5). This does not imply that writers subscribe to the visions presented, but these function as a common point of reference and a way to distinguish between arguments. Indeed, as will be noted in later chapters, works of media resistance seem to be more inspired by literary doomsaying than by empirical studies of how media operate (see also Ch. 7).

Although the novels portray fascinating accounts of media not yet invented, the most interesting aspect is not what they say about the future, but about the time when they were written. The novels were produced in the interwar and early post-war period, an era of immense media expansion, and reflect the need among intellectuals to develop some kind of "working notions" to understand media influences (see Sundet 2012, 14). As Natale and Balbi (2014) argue, "media historians should resist the temptation to validate past media prophecies and instead explore the relationship of these prophecies to the culture of the time in which they were created" (207). The novels are read here as historical sources providing insight into concerns and values at the time (see also Ch. 6 on socio-cultural film studies). Although dystopian narratives visualize and engage with political and cultural debates, the narratives are not "simple reflections of their time or the interests of their audiences; they are deliberate fictional constructs that engages with political and social elements" (Kuhn 1990, 30). Dystopian fiction is located in "a negatively deformed future of our own world" (Baccolini 2003, 115), and uses, in particular, exaggeration as a means of engaging readers and formulate warnings: "If this goes on..." (Gaiman 2013, xii).

In this particular case, the novels exaggerate concerns about early mass media: serial fiction, cinema, radio and comics (Ch. 2). The novels also speculate extensively on the embryonic medium of television and its potentially negative impact. Read as historically grounded warnings, the novels thematize two major dichotomies recurring in media criticism: between print (good) and screen (bad), and between high culture and mass culture. Beyond that, the novels allude to a variety of criticisms and concerns, which has recurred in media resistance until today.

In this chapter, I describe the characters and plots in each novel, as well as the imagined mediascape and characters' relationships with media. Then I turn to what is at stake – how do the novels thematize media impact and the undermining of broadly shared values – loss of morality and culture, enlightenment and community, democracy and health? Since these novels are works of fiction, they do not provide recipes for action as to what to do with the detested media, but they do point to some paths of resistance as more promising than others. In the last part I discuss where hope lies, what kind of action in relation to media are depicted as bringing a possible light in the end of the tunnel.

Brave New World: Porn at the "Feelies"

Brave New World was published in 1932, at the height of public and political concern over mass society and mass culture. The novel is set in a distant future, where inhabitants are basically drowning in pleasure; drugs, scent, games, media, music and pornography. Sex is casual and explicit, children are produced in bottles and true emotions are removed through genetic engineering. In the imagined World State, consumerism is the main religion and citizens substitute the name of industrialist Henry Ford for "Lord" or "Christ"; there is even an alternative bible: "My Life and Work, by Our Ford" (Huxley 2006, 218).

The main male character Bernard Marx is a genetic engineer who is struggling to find his place in society. He starts an affair with the female protagonist Lenina, who is, like other female character in the three novels, portrayed as more superficial than the male characters. The third main figure is John, a "savage" they bring to The World State from an outside reservation; the shortcomings of the state are very much seen through his eyes. John becomes a celebrity, but is deeply disturbed by how modern society has evolved.

The mediascape in *Brave New World* is a mixture of old, new and imagined media. Radio, television, films, music and games are everywhere and constantly used; they represent – in combination with drugs and sex – the main ingredients of a good life. Huxley's novel depicts "synthetic music boxes," "scent organs," electric "skysigns," and electronic games, such as "Electromagnetic Golf." Lenina, who represents a devout media consumer, is exited to tell John about the immense media pleasures awaiting him in the World State: the "lovely music that came out of a box," "all the nice games you could play," "the pictures that you could hear and feel and smell," as well as "the boxes where you could see and hear what was happening at the other side of the world" (128). As the story evolves, Lenina's character continue to represent the sentiments that 1930's media critics warned about. While the male character of Bernard yearns for strong emotions and true passion, the character of Lenina uses media to block out silences as well as conversation: "Let's turn on the radio. Quick!," she says when conversation gets serious, reaching for "the dialling knob on the dashboard" and turning it "at random" (90).

Television, which hardly existed when *Brave New World* was written, is everywhere in the World State. Although some programmes (news, sport) are described, television is very much "flow": "Television was left on, a running tap, from morning till night" (198), and a character constantly watching television is described as "on holiday in some other world" (155). While television prompts passivity, cinema has evolved into virtual reality. The most spectacular media innovation in the novel is the "feelies," huge cinema palaces where image, scent and tactile effects together create an interactive effect. As imagined media, the "feelies" go far beyond the "talkies" (sound movies) of the 1920s and 1930s; feely-characters are described as "more solid-looking than they would have seemed in actual flesh and blood, far more real than reality" (168), synthetic music and scent is pumped out to accentuate the effect, and spectators experience the same sensations as characters by pressing on knobs. When the characters on the screen kiss, the audience can feel the effect:

> "Aa-aah." "Ooh-ah! Ooh-ah!" the stereoscopic lips came together again, and once more the facial erogenous zones of the six thousand spectators in the Alhambra tingled with almost intolerable galvanic pleasure. "Ooh...." (168)

With their interactive features, the futurist media in *Brave New World* are spectacular innovations, their exaggerated features reflecting the criticism of early popular media (Ch. 2). Media keep the population distracted with mindless entertainment, their role similar to drugs, which are also widely available. To indicate the hugely important role played by media in this future society, the production facilities for television, cinema, radio and music are described as enormous: "At Brentford the Television Corporation's factory was like a small town" (62). "The buildings of the Hounslow Feely Studio covered seven and a half hectares" (62). "Then came the Bureau of propaganda by Television, by Feeling picture, and by Synthetic Voice and Music respectively – twenty-two floors of them" (66).

There is also a Department of Writing, but reading is not encouraged; indeed, state institutions use loud noises and electroshock to condition infants to hate books and flowers. All books published before A.F. 150 [A.F = After Ford] have been forbidden (51), as reading comes in the way of consumption and pleasure seeking: "You can't consume much if you sit still and read books" (50). While popular media were criticized as "trash" in the 1930s, Huxley turns the tables and portrays a society where literature is "smut." As Mustapha Mond, a state controller, explains,

> Our civilization has chosen machinery and medicine and happiness. That's why I have to keep these books locked up in the safe. They're smut. (234)

Propaganda and conditioning are crucial to achieve stability, and inhabitants are genetically modified to make them "like their unescapable social destiny" (16). Media are used for brainwashing; from a very young age, children are subject to "sleep-teaching" or "hypnopaedia"; machines repeating the same phrases all night. Adults are indoctrinated through public loudspeakers; when a riot break out the police calms the population with "Synthetic Anti-Riot Speech Number Two (Medium Strength)" (214). The ideas of enlightenment and uplift have vanished; instead, culture and information are streamlined to fit people of different conditioning. Not only the screen media are innovative; newspapers for the lower classes are described as being printed "on khaki paper and in words exclusively of one syllable" (66). Film plots for "feelies" are described as pornographic and stereotypical. Lenina takes John to see a feely where a woman is kidnapped by a "black madman" for "a wildly anti-social tête-à-tête," and later becomes the mistress of all her three rescuers. While Lenina, whose character is conditioned to like this kind of stuff, finds the film "lovely," John the Savage, who has received his education from discarded volumes of Shakespeare in a reservation outside The World State, finds the plot "horrible," "base" and "ignoble." Frustrated, he goes home and reads *Othello* (171).

The media keep the population distracted, but media are also shown to be violent and cruel in their dealings with vulnerable individuals. The portrayal of John's demise is telling; he is first exploited as a celebrity and then victimized by documentary makers and journalists. The book ends with a chilling scene where a fleeing John is hunted down by a pack of reporters, described as "turkey buzzards settling on a corpse" (248). John is basically treated like an animal by the media, we are told that he is put under surveillance by "the Feely Corporation's most expert game photographer," and the documentary about him could be "seen, heard and felt in every first-class feely-palace in Western Europe" (254). After a media witch hunt that turns into an orgy, John hangs himself and the story ends.

Nineteen Eighty-Four: Dictatorship by Telescreen

Published in 1949, deeply marked by the atrocities of World War II, *Nineteen Eighty-four* portrays a world that is more squalid, grey and poor. The events unfold in Airstrip One, formerly known as London, in a world that has been divided into three great super-states constantly at war, reflecting the post-war arms race. The ruling Party, called Ingsoc, with its leader Big Brother, is in full control of society, and has even invented a new language called Newspeak to shape and manipulate the way people think. Thoughtcrime – thinking rebellious thoughts – is the worst of all crimes. Rather than communal bonds, society is held together by hate; the novel depicts media-rich ceremonies organized to stimulate the hating of real and imagined enemies.

The main character Winston works in the Ministry of Truth; his job is to alter historical records to fit the needs of the Party. He is described as increasingly dissatisfied and initiates an illicit affair with a co-worker, Julia, who is more of a happy-go-lucky character than the brooding Winston. Julia and Winston hide in a safe room in the proletarian quarters and begin plotting against the regime, but it turns out that they have been under surveillance the whole time, and they are subsequently captured and tortured.

The media in *Nineteen Eighty-four* are pluralistic, powerful and ubiquitous. All the media of the 1940s are present: radio, film, newspapers and popular fiction, all with exaggerated negative features and depicted as serving the aims of the state. However, what truly makes the story frightening is the imagined medium of the telescreen – an advanced form of two-way television very unlike the early post-war television service that had just started up in Britain when the novel was written (Briggs 1985). The first time the telescreen is introduced is in a scene in Winston's apartment, it is described as "an oblong metal plaque like a dulled mirror which formed part of the surface of the right-hand wall" (2006, 4). We soon learn that screens are everywhere, all party members have them, you find them in all public places, and there are also hidden screens. The telescreen is described as incredible versatile and interactive, it is a television, a surveillance device, a loudspeaker, and a telephone. The screen is "delicate enough to pick up heartbeat" (82) and a "single flicker of the eyes" (39). We are informed that Winston is constantly aware of its presence, seen in phrases such as these: "Winston kept his back turned to the telescreen. It was safer, though, as he well knew, even a back can be revealing" (5). There is no way of knowing when the Thought Police plugs into your individual wire:

> You had to live – did live, from habit that became instinct – in the assumption that every sound you made was overheard, and, except in darkness, every movement scrutinized (5).

The dramatic effect of the constant presence of the telescreen is that of living in a laboratory, a type of experience later recreated in the reality show *Big Brother* from 1999 (see Ytreberg 2003) and also in the film *The Truman Show* (Ch. 6). This is media portrayal at its most dystopic, echoing and pre-echoing concerns about surveillance technologies throughout media history. But the telescreen is not just evil in the way it is used for surveillance, the description of its effects also allude to criticism of media escapism and media as interruption devices. The constant noise from the telescreen makes it impossible to concentrate; a constant outpouring of "facts" about ongoing wars and the victories, military music and patriotic songs, a barrage of statistics proving the success of the Party. Winston's attempts as reflection are constantly disturbed; "with the voice from the telescreen nagging at his ears he could not follow his train of thought further" (107).

Also in *Nineteen Eighty-Four* the media headquarters are impressive, signifying enormous media power. The Ministry of Truth is responsible for all cultural, educational and media production, and completely dwarfs its surroundings: It is "an enormous pyramidal structure of glittering white concrete, soaring up, terrace after terrace, three hundred meters into the air" (2006, 5–6), with 3000 rooms above and same below ground. The task of the Ministry is to supply the citizens of Oceania with "every conceivable kind of information, instruction or entertainment" (44). The culture bears the hallmark of the 1940s popular culture, but taken one-step further, there are "rubbishy newspapers containing almost nothing except sport, crime and astrology, sensationalist five cents novelettes, films oozing with sex," as well as "sentimental songs" produced mechanically on a machine known as a "versificator" (46).

Books are supressed, modified or simply noted as absent. In Winston's flat there is a "shallow alcove" which "had probably been intended to hold bookshelves" (6), but all books printed before 1960 have been destroyed. Short version of classical works by authors such as Chaucer, Shakespeare, Milton and Byron are available in Newspeak, and there is also new fiction, but like the songs, novels are also produced mechanically on novel-writing machines. Alluding to the criticism of standardized mass culture, we are told that "[b]ooks were just a commodity that had to be produced, like jam or bootlaces" (136). Pornography is produced for proletarian youth, with titles such as "Spanking Stories" and "One night in a Girls School," but also these are completely standardized: "They only have six plots but they swap them around a bit" (137).

All forms of creativity are discouraged. Winston is portrayed as taking a great risk by obtaining a notebook, an offence punishable by death or forced-labour camp. The novel details how censorship and propaganda are vital to the stability of the regime. Tellingly, Winston's job is to falsify newspapers such as *The Times* in order to support the current "truth," and the process of alteration is applied to all genres – books, periodicals, pamphlets, posters, leaflets, films, sound-tracks, cartoons, photographs – "to every kind of literature or documentation which might conceivably hold any political or ideological significance" (42).

Meticulous and bureaucratic forms of censorship are combined with violent and brutal media indoctrination. In addition to the annual celebration of "Hate week," a festival centred on enjoyment of hateful media products, gruesome killings of civilians are served up as entertainment in cinema films. Reflecting the atrocities of authoritarian regimes, such as the public trials in Stalinist Soviet in the 1930s, traitors are paraded on television, forced to testify their alleged crimes, live on camera.

Fahrenheit 451: Burning All Books

Published in 1953, only five years after Orwell's dystopia, *Fahrenheit 451* is set in a completely different world. Across the Atlantic, the novel reflects the beginning of the 1950s consumer boom where all sorts of goods became available to the American public: cars, refrigerators, washing machines and not least television sets. However, goods do not bring happiness to characters; life in *Fahrenheit 451* is sterile and cold. There is clearly too much stimulation for a meaningful and healthy life: drinking alcohol, smoking incessantly, driving very fast, consuming media, glaring at huge advertising posters. Suicides are frequent, but victims are quickly back on their feet after being cleaned up by a form of medical vacuum cleaner. In this society, the fire brigade is important for upholding social stability, as their purpose is to locate and burn all books (Fahrenheit 451 is purportedly the temperature at which paper burn).

The main character Guy Montag is a firefighter increasingly at odds with the ethics of his profession. Montag is married to Mildred, another female character represented as a superficial individual; like Lenina in *Brave New World*, she is a passionate media consumer. Montag's journey from loyal book-burner to ardent rebel is stimulated by characters he meets on his way, a young girl named Clarisse, whose innocent questioning opens Montag's eyes to the emptiness of his life, and Faber, a retired English teacher, whose character informs Montag of all that has been lost under the current regime. The story ends with the city being bombed to pieces while Montag flees to join a rebel group, "the book lovers," living on abandoned railway tracks, a post-industrial site of the kind that is often preferred in dystopic fiction.

In *Fahrenheit 451,* reading books is "against the law" (5), and the job of the fire brigade is to hunt down books and burn them. In another ironic inversion of the public criticism in the early and mid-1900s, the aim is also here to obliterate literary culture; the fire station has a list of a million forbidden books and the only permitted books are cartoons and books with pictures. People are killed and taken away to asylum if they do not give up their books; in a crucial scene, an old woman refuses to leave her books and is burned along with them when the firemen arrive. Montag's character is transformed by this event, as he begins to wonder whether there really might be something worthwhile in the books he burns for a living. He begins to steal and hide books, and endangers the life of his wife and acquaintances when he pulls one out and reads when they have company.

While books are burnt, television viewing is encouraged. The novel reflects the criticism of early commercial television in the 1950s, the screen described as "lit with orange and yellow confetti and skyrockets and women in gold-mesh dresses and men in black velvet pulling one-hundred pound rabbits from silver hats" (67). Despite the low-quality content, television is seen as having a strong and direct influence on viewers, as Montag notes:

[Y]ou can't argue with the four-wall televisor. Why? The televisor is "real." It is immediate, it has dimension. It tells you what to think and blasts it in. It *must* be right. It *seems* so right. It rushes you on so quickly to its own conclusions your mind hasn't time to protest, What nonsense! (80)

One reason why television is so influential is sheer size. In *Fahrenheit 451*, Bradbury has added innovative features to the nascent television medium of the 1950s; television is described as "parlor walls"; each screen covering an entire wall in the living room. In Montag's home, we are told that the screens already cover three walls, and although screens are expensive, Mildred's character is nagging him to replace also the fourth wall with a screen. She is presented as deeply bored with real life and argues: "If we had a fourth wall, why it'd be just like the room wasn't ours at all, but a kind of exotic people's rooms" (18). The "parlor walls" are interactive; in one passage Mildred is talking to the television announcer, in another she is depicted as playing a part in an interactive drama. We are told that she has won a competition and received her lines by mail:

> "They write the script with one part missing. It's a new idea. The home-maker, that's me, is the missing part. When it comes time for the missing lines, they all look at me out of three walls and I say the lines. Here, for instance, the man says, 'What do you think of this whole idea, Helen?' And he looks at me sitting here center stage, see? And I say, I say –" She paused and ran her finger under a line on the script. "I think that's fine!" (17–18)

The interactivity alludes to concern over loss of community and family bonds, as Mildred refers to people on television as family members: uncles, aunts, nephews, nieces. When not watching television, Mildred is presented as wearing "seashell radio" (with tiny earplugs, not yet invented when the book was written), which she keeps on all night to block out other impulses. Montag speculates whether he will have to buy himself a radio station to be able to communicate with her, referring to the recurring theme of media as an isolating force. Mildred is portrayed as callous and not even willing to turn off television when Montag is sick: she claims that her favourite show is on, but cannot name it; it is all noise and flow. Montag despises her as well as the television "walls"; he represents the view that television is just "a great thunderstorm of sound," described as turning on a (mental) washing machine (42).

The authoritarian society depicted in *Fahrenheit 451* differs from the World State and Airstrip One; in this society it is not state propaganda that keeps people in the dark. Instead, the novel marks a shift to the post-war era with its explosion in mass culture; everything is made bland to suit the mass market, and there is nothing that can offend minorities or sensitive individuals. Quality culture is dying, instead there are comics and "three-dimensional sex magazines" (55). All plots have been condensed to suit popular taste, in a direct reference to the public debate, Hamlet is described as "a one-page digest in a book that claimed 'now at last you can read all the classics; keep up with your neighbors'" (53). The effect is complete uniformity; the character of Clarisse sums it up when she tells Montag "they all say the same things and nobody says anything different from anyone else" (28).

Yet, the media regime in *Fahrenheit 451* is also depicted as murderous and brutal when the social order is threatened. When Montag flees towards the end of the novel, he is followed by television cameras and media helicopters in a wild chase, not unlike the media frenzy in *Brave New World*. Montag escapes to join a resistance movement, but the state, as well as the television show covering the manhunt, need "a snap ending." So instead of Montag, an innocent victim is caught and killed live on camera, as a brutal form of entertainment. Again, media people are portrayed as literally walking across dead bodies to get what they want.

What is at Stake? Print vs. Screen, Good vs. Bad Literacy

The novels are immensely rich, and could be discussed in the light of almost any aspect of modernity. Yet, the novels portray an unusually large variety of mediascapes, and the media depicted, separately and together, provide comments and reflections on major issues in media resistance. The three novels in their various ways thematize how the media endanger key values of morality, culture, enlightenment, democracy, community and health. Indeed, the media situation in Huxley's World State, Orwell's Airstrip One and Bradbury's sterile city can be seen as exaggerated illustrations as to what could happen if the warnings in media resistance are not heeded and changes not reversed. In this sense, the novels fit the description of dystopia as "a conservative genre": "Its function is to warn readers of the possible outcomes of our present world and entails an extrapolation of key features of contemporary society" (Baccolini 2003, 115).

The explicit sex in *Brave New World*, and the widespread availability of pornography in all three novels, illustrates the concern that media undermine morality; there are pornographic "feelies" at mainstream theatres (*Brave New World*), three-dimensional sex magazines (*Fahrenheit 451*) and standardized pornography plots for proletarian youth (*Nineteen Eighty-Four*). The concern for culture is abundantly illustrated; culture is produced industrially on innovations such as "versificators" and "novel-writing machines" (*Nineteen Eighty-Four*) and commercialization has increased with advertising devices such as "skysigns" (*Brave New World*). Surveillance technology and propaganda have replaced democracy, and state terror, mass culture, genetic engineering or endless consumption has eroded community bonds. In *Fahrenheit 451*, front porches are removed because no one sits and talks at night; in *Brave New World* children are produced in factories and in *Nineteen Eighty-Four* children are spying on their parents on behalf of the state. Media noise block out or prevent communication, concentration and all forms of learning and enlightenment, people hide from each other with "seashell radio" to be listened to with tiny earplugs (*Fahrenheit 451*), or prefer escapist entertainment such as "Electromagnetic Golf" (*Brave New World*).

In addition to illustrate how media erode broadly shared values, the portrayal of media in these novels reflects explicitly on two major dichotomies prevalent in media resistance at the time: between print (good) and screen (bad), and between authentic (high) culture and mass (low) culture.

Although there are many innovations, the most spectacularly dystopic media in the three novels are the screen media. These are definitely a step up from the screen media available in 1932, 1949 and 1953 respectively when the novels were published. All three novels include dystopic visions of the cinema (a place for vulgar and violent entertainment), and indulge in speculating about the effects of the emerging medium of television. In order to depict negative effects, screens are grossly enlarged and exaggerated, there are big screens, small screens and screens everywhere, and the screen media are versatile and powerful. The "feelies" described in *Brave New World* are virtual reality media where all senses are stimulated, the telescreens in *Nineteen Eighty-Four* and "parlor walls" in *Fahrenheit 451* are imagined forms of convergent media with a multitude of functions that make them invasive and disturbing. The good guys in the novels, particularly John the Savage, Winston and Montag, all detest the screen media and try to avoid them, whereas the characters portrayed as more superficial, Lenina and Mildred, enjoy them, reflecting the idea that women were more vulnerable to influence from popular culture (Ch. 2).

In contrast to the fantasies about screen media, the imaginations about traditional forms of literacy in the three novels – poetry, prose, verse, as well as academic books – are of obsolescence and death (see also Natale and Balbi 2014). The novel powerfully illustrates how concerns in media resistance are not just about the presumably bad effects of new media, but about warnings that more valuable media may become extinct. The three authors fantasize spectacularly about the bad things that can happen to books and literacy, such as babies being conditioned with electroshocks to hate books and discarded copies of Shakespeare eaten by mice (*Brave New World*), apartments where bookshelves are replaced with screens and classical works re-written in Newspeak (*Nineteen Eighty-Four*), and the burning of books and persecution of book-lovers (*Fahrenheit 451*). The warning in all three stories is that reading, writing and printing is the very marker of a civilized life, and if books lose ground, the path to apocalypse is short.

As pointed out in Chapter 2, books and printing have also been subject to resistance; the novel was considered "vulgar" when it first appeared (Williams 1958, 306). The three novels innovatively reflect on the criticism of vulgar mass culture and what may happen if warnings such as those advocated by F. R. Leavis and Horkheimer and Adorno are not listened to in their manifestos from 1930 and 1944 respectively. Instead of classical literature, the media that were strongly criticized in the 1930s, 1940s and 1950s have flourished and expanded, and high culture is shown to be destroyed. The two latter novels, *Nineteen Eighty-Four* and *Fahrenheit 451*, also describe comics and abbreviated books, forms that where defended with the argument that they would spread literary knowledge and enhance reading skills. However, both were widely criticized for producing a tepid middle culture destroying the original classics as well as popular taste (see, for example, Wertham 2004, 121; MacDonald 2011, 35).

All three novels refer in various ways to Shakespeare and other classics as a counterpart to the lower forms of media and culture. *Brave New World* has borrowed its title from the Shakespeare play *The Tempest*, John the Savage is self-educated from discarded volumes of Shakespeare, and the novel is littered with Shakespearian references. The two other novels also use the destruction of Shakespearean works as an indication of the rot in society: In *Nineteen Eighty-Four* Shakespeare is rewritten and transformed in Newspeak and in *Fahrenheit 451* Hamlet is reduced to a "one-page digest" (2013, 53). Culture exists, but only for dummies!

The Obliteration of Civilization

The novels reflect on distinctions between print and screen and between good and bad literacy, but go further; they also speculate about the death of entire civilizations. The books portray fully fledged versions of the mass societies critics warned about in the interwar period; there is authoritarian rule instead of democracy, excess and escapism instead of enlightenment, thrash instead of culture, consumerism instead of community, dehumanization instead of morality, and destruction of mental and physical health.

How has this happened? Like other dystopian texts, the novels can be read as warnings but also as explanations: as texts connecting the dots and explaining how societies have ended up in a very bad state. As Baccolini (2003, 115) points out, the dystopian narrative has a complex relationship to history; it often appears as a "critique of history" because it is portraying a deformed future, but history and memory are also crucial to plots. In many dystopian narratives, rulers fear the power of history and keep it hidden from the public since history and memory are "dangerous elements that can give the dystopian citizen a potential instrument of resistance." In all three novels, the main character at some point discovers the "history" of society, or more specifically, how civilization has been obliterated to be replaced by awful dictatorships. The emergence of mass media is crucial in all three explanations.

In *Brave New World*, the role of State controller Mustapha Mond is to explain the emergence of the World State. In the beginning, he claims, there were such things as democracy, liberalism, family life, Christianity and individuality, but after war, destruction and economic collapse everything changed. There was brutal and conscious persecution of dissidents, such as "the gassing of culture fans in the British Museum" (2008, 50), but it was also realized that "you couldn't do things by force" (49). Together with genetic engineering, the mass media did the trick, providing both the tools for propaganda and the distraction that tempted people into pleasure seeking and consumption. When the masses seized political power, happiness rather than truth and beauty mattered:

> You've got to choose between happiness and what people used to call high art. We've sacrificed the high art. We have the feelies and the scent organ instead (220).

In *Nineteen Eighty-Four*, the history of society is partly revealed in a secret manifesto (2006, 191), and this account also points to the combination of brutal repression and mass media propaganda. Continuous warfare was the party's means to uphold scarcity and inequality, but the active obliteration of memory, falsification of truth, narrowing of language and media fakery was also crucial. The account describes the present dictatorship as different from all previous dictatorships; in the past, it was difficult to keep citizens under control, but this changed with new media:

> The invention of print, however, made it easier to manipulate public opinion, and the film and the radio carried the process further. With the development of television, and the technical advance which made it easier to receive and transmit simultaneously on the same instrument, private life came to an end (214).

From this moment, the manifesto says, it was not only possible to enforce "complete obedience to the Will of the State," but also "complete uniformity of opinions on all subjects" (214).

In *Fahrenheit 451*, the history is pieced together through information from Beatty, the Fire Chief, and filled out by Faber, the former English professor whom Montag tracks down. Also in this society, war and destruction played a part, but most important for the evolvement of authoritarianism was the lowering of standards spearheaded by the mass media: "Films and radios, magazines, books levelled down to a sort of paste pudding norm" (51). The sensibilities of various minorities helped to curb free speech. It was a long history of decay, but not the fault of the state:

> It didn't come from the Government down. There was no dictum, no declaration, no censorship, to start with, no! Technology, mass exploitation, and minority presence carried the trick, thank God. Today, thanks to them, you can stay happy all the time, you are allowed to read comics, the good old confessions, or trade journals (55).

Although the details vary, all three authors describe mass communications as vital mechanisms in creating authoritarian societies, not necessarily causes, but instruments in the hands of the evil rulers. But they go further; the growth of the mass media is paralleled by a decline in vital institutions of civil society and the failure of intellectuals to protect the values of enlightenment, democracy and culture.

Specifically, the expansion of media parallels a forceful decline in science and the humanities: Scientists are exiled (*Brave New World*), there is no word for science in Newspeak (*Nineteen Eighty-Four*) and in *Fahrenheit 451* we are told that "the last liberal arts college shut down for lack of students and patronage" forty years earlier (71). History is meticulously and actively falsified, dropped from the curriculum and ridiculed: in *Brave New World* society is run according to the Henry Ford's dictum: "History is Bunk!" Language fare no better, most world languages are dead (*Brave New World*), English and spelling are ignored (*Fahrenheit 451*), and in *Nineteen Eighty-Four*, the whole of the English language, Oldspeak, is destroyed. In all three novels, intellectuals are depicted as critical, but not sufficiently vigilant when warning signs were flashing, and many academics have sold out to the regimes; brilliant scientists work with genetic manipulation in *Brave New World* and philologists are busy creating Newspeak in *Nineteen Eighty-Four*. In *Fahrenheit 451*, teachers have completely succumbed to media and education consists of "TV-class" or "film teacher" (27).

Indeed, in all three novels there has been a transfer from classical disciplines to media and communication disciplines and professions. The main characters all work in what may broadly be labelled "the media," although in a perverted sense: In *Brave New World* Bernard Marx is accredited as "the Professor of Feelies in the College of Emotional Engineering" (156), in *Nineteen Eighty-Four*, Winston is falsifying newspapers, and Montag in *Fahrenheit 451* burns books. Those who work with media are not to be trusted, and part of the liberation process is to get out of this kind of work.

WHAT TO DO? WHERE DOES HOPE LIE?

While cultural and political manifestos are about mobilizing for action, no such explicit demands can be claimed of fiction. Yet, it is interesting to see if the authors point to a way out. Having created these awful dystopias, do Huxley, Orwell and Bradbury allow the reader any hope? What kind of action is pointed to as potentially leading humanity to a better place and what kind of hope is envisaged for characters?

In all three stories, there are parallel narratives of repression and resistance. A counter-narrative is developed "as the dystopian citizen moves from apparent contentment into an experience of alienation and resistance" (Baccolini and Moylan 2003, 5). The re-appropriation of language, memory, history and forms of education lost or prohibited are crucial tools in the protagonists' actions to instigate social change. Yet, the actions are not always successful in terms of leading in a new direction.

The bleakest story is *Nineteen Eighty-Four*. Winston hopes that the proletarians will revolt (2006, 274), but the destiny of the main characters, who are tortured, brainwashed and coerced to love Big Brother, indicates that Winston's thought are probably feeble fantasies. The only hope lies in the possibility that autonomous subjects may continue to emerge, despite the appalling conditions (Ytreberg 2003).

The two other novels are more hopeful. Both in *Brave New World* and in *Fahrenheit 451*, enclaves on the margins of society are described with remnants of traditional civilization. In *Brave New World* there is the savage reservation where they still have some books and breed children the natural way, as well as the islands where writers and scientists are exiled. Hope lie in the character of Helmholz, a friend of Bernard's, who is sent to the Falklands; he embraces the idea of being sent to a cold place, since this will give him the best opportunities to write. Helmholz is portrayed as desperately sick of writing state-approved propaganda rhymes; he wants to write "piercingly" (70); he is inspired by Shakespeare, which John the Savage has taught him. The controller Mustafa Mond, who is himself an intellectual who has sold out to the regime, describes exile very positively to Helmholz; the islands are where they send "the most interesting people":

> All the people who aren't satisfied with orthodoxy, who've got independent ideas of their own. Every one, in a word, who's any one. I almost envy you, Mr. Watson (227).

In *Fahrenheit 451*, hope is in the "book people," an illicit group living on abandoned railway tracks, each memorizing a classical work to conserve heritage and knowledge. Many are former academics; ironically one of the first Montag meets is Dr. Simmon's from UCCL, "a specialist in Ortega Y'Gasset" (143), the mass society theorist who predicted in 1930 that the masses would destroy everything of quality (Ch. 2) The book people are the closest one can come to fictional heroes from the humanities. They think of people as "book jackets" and their hopes are timeless and cogently expressed (146–147):

> And when the war's over some day, some year, the books can be written again, the people will be called in, one by one, to recite what they know and

we'll set it up in type until another Dark Age, when we might have to do the whole damn thing over again. But that's the wonderful thing about man; he never gets so discouraged or disgusted that he gives up doing it all over again, because he knows very well it is important and *worth* the doing.

Fittingly, it is by removing oneself from the authoritarian state and the mass media, and seeking refuge in traditional literacy and writing, that humanity is offered a glimmer of hope. And in *Fahrenheit 451*, we actually come close to a "happy ending." In the last passages, society is obliterated in a great blast, and when the novel ends, it looks like only the book people have survived.

Open Access This chapter is licensed under the terms of the Creative Commons Attribution 4.0 International License (http://creativecommons.org/licenses/by/4.0/), which permits use, sharing, adaptation, distribution and reproduction in any medium or format, as long as you give appropriate credit to the original author(s) and the source, provide a link to the Creative Commons license and indicate if changes were made.

The images or other third party material in this chapter are included in the book's Creative Commons license, unless indicated otherwise in a credit line to the material. If material is not included in the book's Creative Commons license and your intended use is not permitted by statutory regulation or exceeds the permitted use, you will need to obtain permission directly from the copyright holder.

CHAPTER 4

"Get a Life!" Anti-Television Agitation and Activism

Abstract No modern medium has been detested as much as television. The chapter reviews key works by Mary Whitehouse, Marie Winn, Jerry Mander and Neil Postman deeming television to be a cause of social ills in the 1960s, 1970s and 1980s. Television was seen to undermine democracy, community and enlightenment, obstructing a moral lifestyle, and impairing mental and physical health. The chapter discusses collective action against television through movements such as TV-Free America, the British White dot and Adbusters. While anti-television activism did not inspire a general rejection of television, TV-Turnoff Week from the mid-1990s became a way for organizations, professions, communities and individuals to demonstrate their resentment and point to television as an explanation for social change to the worse.

Keywords Television · Tv-turnoff · Tv-boycott · Idiot box · Passive viewing

THE CHIEF CULPRIT

Max Horkheimer and Theodor W. Adorno had not had much chance to watch television when they published *The culture industry: Enlightenment as mass deception*, in 1944, but they had heard about it. Describing it as "a synthesis of

---
*is used throughout the book to indicate my translation.

radio and film," they expected its effect to be "enormous" and that it would drastically "intensify the impoverishment of aesthetic matter" (1997, 124). Horkheimer and Adorno echoed sentiments expressed in other texts from the same period, including views attributed to characters in dystopic fiction such as *Brave New World, Nineteen Eighty-Four* and *Fahrenheit 451* (Ch. 3).

Narratives of warning are an important part of media history and inform us about expectations at a time when few have first-hand experience with a new medium. Yet, television scepticism did not disappear once the medium matured. Instead, narratives of warning gave way to narratives of explanation, pointing to television as a cause of social change to the worse. In the post-war decades of massive social transformation, television became "the chief culprit in the alleged decline and fall of contemporary culture" (Brantlinger 1983, 19).

This chapter is about writers and activists who did not become convinced that television was a good thing. Since television continued to grow in importance, resistance can be studied as a lost cause; resisters are just moralists, luddites and pessimists who never seem to catch up. To anti-television writers or activists, however, it is the television crowd who does not get it. As argued in a campaign for *TV-turnoff week* (2012), turnoff is not about saying "no" but saying "yes":

> National TV-turnoff Week is about having more fun and turning "on" your life. It's an opportunity to rediscover the wide range of activities that exist when one unplugs from the sedentary, image-based, simplistic and commercial world of television.

This chapter provides insight into television resistance through a discussion of selected writers and cases. The first part of the chapter discusses resistance literature; specifically four writers who were widely read at the time and illustrate a broad range of concerns about television. Mary Whitehouse was a British schoolteacher who organized a major television-critical movement from the 1960s in the UK, whereas Jerry Mander, Neil Postman and Marie Winn separately and together inspired television resistance in the US and internationally in the 1970s and 1980s. The chapter explores how central values in media resistance, for morality and culture, enlightenment and democracy, community and health (Chs. 1 and 2), emerge in television-critical arguments and actions, and points to the rise of new metaphors, such as "couch potato" and "the idiot box," implying that viewers were lazy and the content harmful and stupid.

In the second part of the chapter, I discuss resistance movements; organized action to reduce the importance of television. Based on websites, media interviews, statements and documents, the ideologies and methods adopted by *TV-Free America, Adbusters, White dot* and *TV-turnoff week* are discussed from the mid-1990s until the early 2000s. The emphasis in this chapter is not on reception of new media, but rather on resistance to an established medium; providing an alternative to the usual narrative where scepticism and fear give way to acceptance.

Historical and social conditions shaped television resistance and television evolved differently in different contexts (see, for example, Smith and Paterson 1998). In particular, there are differences between the US, adopting a commercial model for broadcasting, and the European public service tradition (see also Ch. 2 on radio). In this chapter I draw predominantly on examples and cases from the US and UK, with some examples from Scandinavia and elsewhere. With public service television and a lower level of consumption in Europe there is less of a history of anti-television action once the medium matured; anti-television activism had more support in the US, where the commercial system gave protesters more to despise. However, both agitators and forms of activism travel across borders and operate in different national contexts.

Although it is not easy to draw a firm line, two positions emerge in the material discussed. On the one hand, there are those who reacted to television's content, genres and functions, but believed that the medium could be improved. On the other hand, there are those who saw television as irredeemable, and advocated its elimination.

Cleaning Up Television

British schoolteacher Mary Whitehouse began her campaign to "clean up" television in 1964. Whitehouse, who would become one of the twentieth century's most avid media protesters, initially held high hopes for television. But soon anger and disappointment set in; this was Britain in the sixties and a more permissive climate had begun to influence the public broadcasting ethos.

As one of the early examples that awakened her, Whitehouse refers to a discussion on pre-marital sex on the BBC in March 1964. Several speakers indicated that premarital sex was not immoral if certain conditions were met. This had a direct impact on the girls in her class, who, according to

Whitehouse, instantly learned that it was acceptable to have intercourse when engaged to be married:

> This made a tremendous impression on me.... Had a few adults... been able to swing the thinking of a generation and manage to destroy in a few minutes their traditional concepts of right and wrong? (1967, 16)

During the summer of 1963, Whitehouse contacted broadcasters as well as the Minister of Health and leading members of the church. She was courteously received by all, and returned to the school feeling "that things would surely improve" (1967, 19). What happened instead was that the BBC launched a series of plays that autumn which, as Whitehouse saw it, reached "a level of depravity not seen before or – with some notable exceptions – since" (1967, 19). Disillusioned and angry, Whitehouse drafted a manifesto which became the basis for a mass mobilization: "Women's organisations, magistrates, church leaders, feature writers, public figures and private people all joined in" (1967, 19). The campaign is detailed in her 1967 book, *Cleaning up TV. From protest to participation* and in the autobiography *Quite Contrary* (1993, see also Tracey and Morrison 1979).

For Whitehouse, a devout Christian, what was at stake was morality, that is, fundamental questions of right and wrong. Moral campaigns against television had much in common with earlier protests against popular fiction, cinema and comics (Ch. 2), and later protests against videos, games and online pornography (Chs. 5 and 6). Moral campaigners of various inclinations do not necessarily dislike the media, but campaign to get them back on track – back to the role of offering moral guidance. The manifesto of *Clean-up TV* begins: "We women of Britain believe in a Christian way of life," and goes on to demand that the BBC should produce programmes "which build character instead of destroying it, which encourage and sustain faith in God and bring Him back to the hearth of our family and national life" (Whitehouse 1967, 23).

What distinguished Whitehouse from other TV-critical campaigners was her organizational talents and exceedingly high number of supporters. The campaign with 7000 activists was run from a bedroom in her house (1967, 42). The manifesto was distributed in steelworks, factories, schools and hospitals, it was read aloud in churches all over Britain, and gained nearly half a million signatures. Whitehouse received more than 35,000 letters of concern, enjoyed strong support from the police and was invited to meet Pope Paul VI (1993, 37). Whitehouse travelled all over Europe, the US and Australia, inspiring supporters and establishing local chapters. The campaign turned into the *Viewer's and Listeners' Association* in 1965, which went on to protest against other media and genres (Whitehouse 1993, Tracey and Morrison 1979). Among their victories they counted a law against "video nasties" in 1984 (Barker 1984b, ch. 6) and the establishment of a Broadcasting Standards Commission from 1996.

Despite the strong reactions to television, Whitehouse did not encourage abstention. On the contrary, close monitoring by hundreds of volunteers provided the programme samples that were brought to politicians, broadcasters and courts as ground for protest. Whitehouse represents a type of television resistance that primarily reacted to offensive content and put pressure on authorities to impose restrictions; but as her campaign expanded, so did also the liberalizing forces. "As I write I can already hear the snorts of indignation from the 'freedom for television' advocates," Whitehouse commented on the growing anti-censorship lobby (1967, 17). Whitehouse was met with formidable opposition and a range of negative labels were attributed to her; but in contrast to many later activists, who struggled to show that they were not simple-minded moralists, Whitehouse took a more confrontational stance. "It is sometimes suggested that we are 'non-intellectual' and 'unimaginative'," she wrote, and continued, "Well, what if we are? Have we any less right to make our views known?" (1967, 29).

Mander and the Elimination of Television

On the other side of the Atlantic, Jerry Mander had started out a successful advertising executive, but after a while, he reports that he "began to realize a kind of hollowness in myself" (Mander 1978, 15). The 1960s provided opportunities for getting involved in social and political protests, and with his skills in advertising, Mander aided activists wanting to use television for beneficial purposes. However, for Mander himself, this only led to disappointment. Slowly he came to realize that television was irredeemable, in his words, it could not be used to spread "prosocial values" (36–39). In *Four arguments for the elimination of television* (1978, first publ. 1977), an almost 400 page long manifesto littered with references to social decay – *Brave New World, Nineteen Eighty-Four* and *Fahrenheit 451* are all points of reference – Mander argues that television will destroy democracy and lead to authoritarian rule.

The historical context for Mander's criticism was US television at the height of the network era. Whereas television everywhere drew criticism of triviality, the US system alienated more with its blatant commercialism and "lowest common denominator" programing (Giersing 1986). Already in 1961, the Head of the US Federal Communication Commission proclaimed US television "a vast wasteland" for its endless procession of game shows, westerns, formula comedies, violence, murder and sadism (Minow 1961). Mander's vocabulary resembles Marxism in some parts, he argues that television drives us into a capitalist consumer culture and creates false needs (126). Television is an agent of indoctrination and brainwashing: "We accept whatever comes. ...We have lost control of our minds" (112). However, the analysis is not limited to political or economic concerns; he believes the technology itself to be at fault (261):

> Television's highest potential is advertising. This cannot be changed. The bias is inherent in the technology.

According to Mander, television's built-in demand for polarization and dramatization implied that it was unable to convey subtlety; too many crucial pieces "fall through the filter" (323). Mander lists what he sees as 33 inherent biases in the television technology, including "1. Violence is better TV than nonviolence," "9. Superficiality is easier than depth," "13. Lust is better television than satisfaction," "14. Competition is inherently more televisual than cooperation" and "21. The bizarre always gets more attention on television than the usual" (323–328).

In media studies, the view that the medium's technology is more important than content, is often labelled "medium theory" (Meyrowitz 1985, 16; Croteau and Hoynes 2012, 299). First among the medium theorists is Marshall McLuhan (1968) known for the dictum "the medium is the message" and theories of how new media reshaped social life. Although McLuhan was a media and technology enthusiast, similar ideas were discussed at the time with a dystopian slant. For example, the German philosopher Günther Anders in 1956 formulated ten theses about how the broadcasting technology would enslave humanity: "[B]y virtue of their fixed structure and functions" the broadcasting media created a pseudo-reality, he argued, where we would live our lives as "minors and subordinates" (Anders 1956).

In academic accounts, this type of thinking is routinely classified as technological determinism; overstating technology and understating agency (Croteau and Hoynes 2012, 290). Yet, social and political manifestos like Anders' and Mander's are not academic studies, and their most interesting characteristic is not where they can be placed on a simple dichotomy. Instead, it is interesting how they eclectically draw on a variety of concerns and observations in order to explain why media are bad. In addition to his overarching concern that democracy is under threat, Mander sees television to destroy mental and physical health, based on stories about viewers who have turned "sick, crazy, mesmerized" (157), he discusses television inability to convey art and culture (272–273) and laments the loss of community: "The extended family is gone and neighbourhood community gatherings are increasingly the exception to the rule" (254). Mander himself was no fan of McLuhan; he felt that McLuhan's thinking "did not help us very much," calling his terminology "talk show patter" and "wordplay" which "became the basis of hundreds of conferences and thousands of cocktail party debates" (30).

Huxley was Right: Postman and Amusing Ourselves to Death

Neil Postman, educator and self-professed "media ecologist," sold more than 200,000 copies of his 1985 anti-television manifesto, *Amusing Ourselves to Death* (2005a, figures according to Wikipedia). The book began as a lecture at the 1984 Frankfurt Book Fair commemorating Orwell's dystopian vision, but Postman argued that Orwell did not get it right after all. Television did not lead to authoritarian rule; instead, television was realizing the Huxleyan warning of turning public life into entertainment (3–4). "Television does not ban books, it simply displaces them" (141), says Postman in a catching phrase, although a phrase which stretches Huxley's narrative. In *Brave New World* books are not merely "displaced," as we have seen (ch. 3); instead Huxley depicts a society where literary culture is forcefully repressed, there is widespread censorship, and babies are conditioned with electrical shocks to resist books.

Postman pays tribute to McLuhan for pointing out that function is more important than content (8), but is no fan of Mander, calling his book in passing for a "straight Luddite position" (158). Postman is not alarmed by the threat of authoritarianism – what he sees as the Orwellian dystopia – but television's ability to turn everything into entertainment. What is at risk for Postman is the entire enlightenment project; television undermines reason, rationality and print culture, the very foundations of society. "Most of our modern ideas about the uses of the intellect were formed by the printed word, as were our ideas about education, knowledge, truth and information" (29), he writes. But in the 1980s The Age of Television had completely succeeded The Age of Typography. Under the governance of the printing press, public discourse was "coherent, serious and rational," but under the governance of television it had become "shrivelled and absurd" (16), "getting sillier by the minute" (24).

Postman's message is classical pro-print, anti-screen. And while Mander had tried to use television for beneficial purposes, Postman sees no purpose in trying. But the conclusions are the same: television is irredeemable. Postman speaks specifically against news, current affairs, educational television and public broadcasting programmes such as *60 Minutes* and *Sesame Street*; instead of trying to fill television with good content his view is: The worse the better! He asserts that television (159)

> serves us most usefully when presenting junk-entertainment; it serves us most ill when it co-opts serious modes of discourse – news, politics, science, education, commercial, religion – and turns them into entertainment packages. We would all be better off if television got worse, not better.

Postman's book was extremely successful; it was translated into a dozen languages, including German, Indonesian, Chinese and Scandinavian languages (Postman 2005b, viii). Postman himself travelled the world at a time – the mid-1980s – when the broadcasting monopolies were toppling and commercialization and globalization hotly debated. In these debates, there was demand for voices to condemn commercial broadcasting and defend public service, and it testifies to Postman's flexibility that he adjusted his arguments to fill the role. On a visit to Norway in 1987, he warns against the introduction of advertising on television, this would "be equal to meeting a slow death as unenlightened people"* (Aftret and Jacobsen 1987). Apparently, the idea that television ought to get worse not better, and that commercial television and junk-entertainment was better than public and educational television, did not apply overseas.

WINN AND THE PLUG-IN-DRUG

Marie Winn, a translator, author, birdwatcher and an advocate for protecting wildlife, based her bestselling manifesto *The Plug-In Drug* (1980, first publ. 1977) on a huge amount of testimonials. Winn herself had been inspired to engage with television after observing her children watching *Flintstone* and *I Love Lucy*, noting that "the children's chins and jaws were hanging limply, their eyes glazed over and expressions vacant"* (Shulins 1987). Although she later claims that her purpose was not "to promote its elimination altogether" (Winn 2002, x), her argument is that television is not a symptom of social ills, but the actual cause:

> There are two ways to consider television in our society. Its use and overuse may be seen as symptoms of other modern ills: alienation, dehumanization, apathy, moral vacuum. Or one can regard the television set at as a pathogen, a *source* of such symptoms (1980, 245).

Like Mander and Postman, Winn is critical of attempts to improve television or using it for beneficial purposes (6). She ridicules researchers for measuring the effects of specific content, when what matters is "[t]he very nature of the television experience" (3). Although Winn sees television itself to be the problem, her concerns differ from Mander's and Postman's, and she calls McLuhan "apocalyptic" (3).

To Winn, television destroys mental and physical health, and undermines community, particularly its key element: the family. Life with television is life without stimulation, with television we see a reversal of human development, she draws parallels with animals raised in cages and children raised by animals. Television is addictive, like drugs and alcohol, and impairs cognition, visualization and concentration. To Winn, the changes of lifestyle in the 1960s and 1970s are only negative, and probably all due to television:

> There is no *proof* that television viewing is seriously related to declining verbal abilities, to the appearance of a new life style, to alarming trends such as drug use and drug abuse among increasing numbers of young people. But

when all the elements of the puzzle are brought together and examined, television seems seriously implicated in the outcome of the first generation that grew up under its influence. And something is odd about the new generation, something is wrong somehow... (115–116).

Winn is also eclectic in her concerns; in addition to concerns for community and mental health she points to loss of moral guidance and enlightenment; television impairs reading and particularly the crucial ability of "inner picture-making" (1980, 64). However, what distinguished Winn from other critics is her practical approach; she proposes concrete methods to tackle the problem.

A Call to Action?

Those who believed that television could be improved, like Whitehouse, could rely on a trusted arsenal of campaigning methods. Those who believed it to be irredeemable faced bigger challenges. Mander, Postman and Winn were no fans of teaching media literacy, which was favoured by many scholars and critics as a response to increased media use and content perceived to be problematic (see, for example, McGrane and Gunderson 2010). Yet, they were battling with what to propose instead.

Since television subverts democracy, the democratic process should ideally be used to subvert it, Mander writes (1978, 353). But he is not optimistic. Since television colonizes the mind, people would not vote for anyone suggesting abolition. In a postscript called "Impossible thoughts," he recounts the reactions when he tells people that television should be abolished:

> "I couldn't agree with you more", would be the invariable response, "but you don't really expect to succeed, do you?" (347)

In an introduction to the 25th anniversary edition, Postman's son, Andrew, calls his father's book "a call to action" (2005b, xiii). However, the original text does not really make it clear what action Postman recommends. He discusses and rejects several methods and describes "insurmountable difficulties" in suggesting "remedies for the affliction" (2005a, 158). Postman asserts that "[m]any civilized nations limit by law the amount of hours television may operate and thereby mitigate the role television plays in public life," yet mentions no country or legal measure (158). He toys with the idea that satire may demonstrate how ridiculous television is, but notes sadly that performers would become celebrities and "television would have the last laugh" (162). His best hope is in education, but he laments that teachers are not teaching children to "distance themselves" (163). So this solution is also "desperate" and "naive" in Postman's own words (162).

Winn battles less with the question of what to do. Part IV of her book titles "No television" and contains reports and testimonies from people who have given up television, including a report from an experiment she initiated in Denver in 1974 where families were encouraged to turn off television for a month (1980, 220–229). This was presumably the first organized TV-boycott in the US (Winn 1987, xiv), but others were soon to follow (Fang 2015, 7; Winn 1987, 131–133). The event that gained the most publicity, both in the US and overseas, was a month long turnoff initiated by the Library Council of Farmington in 1984, where more than a thousand residents took part (Winn 1987, 132). Librarian Nancy de Salvo, the chief organizer, appeared by phone on *The Letterman Show,* where she was offered a bribe to turn her television back on, but did not give in (Freedman 1998). The event is discussed by Postman (2005a, 158–159) and cited as an explicit source of inspiration for *TV-Free America* (Hirsch 1998).

Inspired by these events, Winn publishes a second book in 1987 – an action manual called *Unplugging the Plug-In drug: The "No TV Week" Guide.* The book advocates consumer boycotts of television, in the same way as activists initiated boycotts in other businesses and markets (Friedman 1999). The book contains everything needed to organize a television boycott: sample invites to meetings, press releases, pledges to sign for participants, notes to speakers etc. In addition to practical advice, the book demonstrates awareness of potentially negative reactions and warns against moralizing. For example, "How to Organize and Run a Parent's Meeting About Television" starts with a warning that "the tone of your presentation is crucial; a 'We're all in this together' attitude is more persuasive than a 'I am here to make you see the light' approach" (1987, 179).

TV-Free America

In the 1990s, activists on both sides of the Atlantic responded to the call. Inspired by literature and boycotts, as well as their own negative experiences, the time had come for collective action to rid the world of television. *TV-Free America*, founded in 1994, was the first to institutionalize annual *TV-turnoff weeks*, followed by networks such as Canadian-based *Adbusters* and British *White dot*. As stated on the website in 2002, the network was

> dedicated to the belief that we all have the power to determine the role that television plays in our lives. Rather than waiting for others to make "better" TV, we can turn it off and reclaim time for our families, our friends and for ourselves (TV-Turnoff 2002a).

The two founders of *TV-Free America*, Henry Labalme and Matt Pawa, are described in interviews as environmentalists and intellectuals, a political scientist and lawyer respectively. Both loved TV at a young age, but turned against it at university. "Once you've taken an extended break" from television, Labalme says in a later interview: "you realize this is so much better. I'm accomplishing so much more.... You wonder, 'How did I ever have time?' to watch so much television" (Hirsch 1998).

The idea to set up a nation-wide network came when Labalme and Pawa were housemates in Georgetown, Washington, in their twenties. Their long conversations "about the decline of literacy, the rise in consumerism and the degradation of the environment kept coming back to television" as a root source of many environmental, social and political problems (cited from Johnson 1996).

The two organizers took time out of their jobs to start *TV-free America* and initiate the first National *TV-turnoff week* in 1995 (Johnson 1996). The group immediately attracted publicity. As TV-resisters, Pawa and Labalme refused to appear on talk shows and declined invitations to CNN (Dundjerski 1997). But they willingly appeared in newspapers and embraced the embryonic Internet – filling their website with arguments, statistics, alternative activities and joyful testimonies from the TV-free. They also credited inspirational figures: On the advisory board were Mander, Winn and Postman, as well as DeSalvo, the librarian who had organized the turnoff in Farmington (TV Turnoff 2000a).

Although the founders were eager that the organization should not appear self-righteous, they did not wish to compromise. To *TV-Free*

America, short-term turnoffs was a means of getting rid of television altogether. When the first national turnoff was organized in 1995, a primary goal was announced of cutting viewing time in half in ten years (Hirsch 1998). They also take an explicit stand against movements trying to improve content or promoting media literacy as a sufficient solution. In a 1998 interview, Labalme states that "people have been arguing for years about 'good' television vs. 'bad' television – and accomplished very little." Arguing for better television "is like trying to cure alcoholism by switching to better whiskey," he says, attributing the quote to Marie Winn (Hirsch 1998).

TV-Free America also takes charge with people who think that some television, such as documentaries or public broadcasting, is somehow acceptable: One question in a QA-page is: "Is all TV bad? What about the Discovery Channel or PBS?" *TV-Free America* answers:

> All TV is passive, sedentary and non-experiential. Most viewers tend to watch show after show – not individual programs. Instead of watching a documentary about birds, go out (with binoculars if you have them) and see how many real birds you can identify in your neighborhood (TV Turnoff 2002c).

Television is rejected because of its flow character (see Williams 2008), but all forms of television and all forms of watching are bad. In a 1998 interview a spokesperson said that "no matter what people do instead of watching the tube – whether they write a letter to the president, wash the dog or do a rain dance – they will be better off" (Dundjerski 1997). Yet, the network wants the message to be positive and not allude to cultural pessimism or moralism. "The idea's not to beat people over the head with this idea that TV is bad for them, that it's rotting their brain, that it's destroying their communities," Labalme says in a 1997 interview: "But to say, try life with a little less TV and a little more time, and you'll have more fun" (Dundjerski 1997). The network actively confronts the image of resisters as sour and fearful Luddites on the outskirts of society. Rather, it is the television viewer who is isolated:

> People say TV unites us, especially big events such as the Superbowl… But that is a myth. If you want diversity, walk around your block and if you want community, talk to your neighbors. TV is an isolating medium (Labalme in Freedman 1998).

Later *TV-Free America* would put a quote on the website from Ray Bradbury commenting in 2007 on why he wrote *Fahrenheit 451* (see also Ch. 3). Rejecting interpretations that the story was a political protest in the McCarthy era, Bradbury stated "I wasn't worried about censorship. I was worried about people being turned into morons by TV" (Kaufman 2007; Rothman 2007). The quote suits the mood of *TV-free America* well – they do not fear Orwell's Big Brother, they just do not want people to be "morons." The quote also testifies to smugness among abstainers and the belief that non-viewers are smarter. Winn notes how non-viewers felt "evangelistic" (1980, 243) and that "a feeling of pride that sometimes borders on the self-satisfied" prevailed among no-television families (240, see also Krcmar 2009).

GRASS-ROOT ACTIVISM AND PROFESSIONAL SUPPORT

TV-free America claimed to be "a grassroot project that works" (TV Turnoff 2002a). Their main activity, organizing *TV-turnoff week*, was done in collaboration with local organizers, schools, clubs, community organizations, religious congregations, shops and businesses. According to *TV-Free America*, there were 5000 local organizers in 1995 (Singer 1996), growing to 35,000 in 1998 (Freedman 1998). Many bought "turn-off kits" at $10 apiece with tips for what to do, posters and bumper stickers, ready-made leaflets and other campaign material (TV Turnoff 2002b).

Teachers and their allies: professors, librarians and organizations promoting literacy, were among the more ardent supporters. According to organizers, turnoffs were organized in 50,000 schools in 2000 (TV Turnoff 2000c). Press clippings and websites contain numerous examples of activities. Such is a typical report, this one from the second turnoff week in 1996 (Johnson 1996):

> In the Inland Northwest, schools promoted the idea with newsletters and posters. Spokane's Jefferson Elementary had a daily prize drawing for students who brought in coupons listing what they did instead of watching TV. Few schools did as much as Windsor Elementary, where parent volunteer Barb Brock, a recreation management professor at EWU, planned activities. She organized a teddy-bear story night, poster contest and distributed information to classes. Nine-year-old Nick Gaddy's family turned off two TVs and borrowed an old record player from the school. "We listened to records," he said. "The big, black ones."

There is plenty of nostalgia, plenty of community and plenty of fun. Turnoff-reports are littered with ice-cream festivals, parties, picnics and rewards (Johnson 1996). School officials go to great length to please non-watching pupils and families: One principal spent an entire day on the roof to reward participants (Dundjerski 1997), another let students cut and spike his hair as a reward for staying off television (Kelly 1996). Similar reports emerge from religious congregations and local communities. One typical local report features the 1999 turnoff at the Mandarin United Methodist Church where sixty families were handed red ribbons to tape across their TV-sets, and the event was celebrated with a church picnic (McAlister 1999).

Not all were in it for the fun, however. Paralleling local activism was massive endorsement of TV-turnoff week from state and nation-wide organizations. A 2002 list on the website named seventy endorsers, of which most were national professional bodies (2002e). All major US educational and medical organizations endorsed the campaign, so did also religious bodies, state and local councils, community organizations, and organizations for arts, the environment, sports and the outdoors.

In January 1995, *TV-Free America* approached the US Catholic Conference of Bishops resulting in a major victory (Johnson 1996). In his March 10th address in St. Peter's Square, Pope John Paul II called upon Catholics all over the world to engage in a TV-fast during Lent (Christus rex 1996):

> In many families the television seems to substitute, rather than facilitate, dialogue among people...A type of "fast" also in this area could be healthy.

Public authorities used *TV-turnoff week* to aid their case. Over the years, the event gained support from a majority of US governors (Freedman 1998; Dundjerski 1997). In 1999, the week was boosted by the support of the US Surgeon General David Satcher; noting that "obesity levels are at epidemic proportions for both children and adults," he wanted to "challenge Americans to break free of TV." Satcher visited an elementary school where he distributed a "Surgeon General's prescription for Less TV," encouraging students to tape them to screens at home. He was accompanied by the Under-Secretary of Agriculture for Food, Nutrition and Consumer Services, Shirley Watkins, who encouraged Americans to "get up off the couch" and "shelve the remote." Echoing the goals of *TV-Free*

America, she suggested beginning with a cut of fifty per cent in viewing time (TV Turnoff 2000b).

The organizers themselves pointed to the wide appeal across political, religious and other divides: "We've got the political left and the political right," Labalme said in a 1996 interview, emphasizing the fluid and flexible ideology:

> We say turn off the TV for your own reasons: because there's too much sex and violence, because it leads to couch potato-ness, which is a health issue, or because people aren't going to church and losing touch with spirituality (cited from Johnson 1996).

One advantage of the TV-free cause was its adaptability: not only did it appear to serve different values; different organizations could also fit it into their calendar of events and tailor it to their own particular cause or action plan.

Turnoff Travels

Turnoff spread – to Canada, Australia and New Zealand, Latin America, and to Britain, Scandinavia and elsewhere. In 2002 *TV-Free America* claimed to have sister organizations in more than twenty countries (TV-turnoff 2002d).

The Vancouver-based network of "culture-jammers," *Adbusters*, supported the cause from the beginning. While many activists shunned appearing on television, *Adbusters* produced anti-television commercials. The first was broadcast on CNN – the only network that would take it – on 22 April 1999 (Adbusters 2002). The commercials are brief television horror stories. For example, the 2007 commercial shows a young man's head trapped inside a set (Adbusters 2007).

In 2001 turnoff is introduced to Sweden and in 2002 to Norway. Television turnoff week did not make deep inroads into the Nordic countries with their tradition of public service broadcasting and their viewing figures the lowest in Europe (Syvertsen et al. 2014). In Scandinavia, boycotting television for a week, instead served to demonstrate the fluidity of the cause and how a television protest could serve different purposes. For example, to the Norwegian Christian media watch organization, *Familie og Medier*, turnoff was about consumerism, bad role models and contemplation over "how much space the media take in our lives"* (Ulveseth 2005). To the teachers and students at the school of

Moe in Southern Norway, turnoff was about reading and switching television for books (Stulen 2005). To the municipality of Melhus in mid-Norway, television turnoff week in 2006 was all about culture. A weeklong arts festival with local performers provided the council an opportunity to launch its new online arts portal, their motto being "to turn off television and get out" to watch local performers* (Refsnes 2006).

In Britain, there were more militant activists. *White dot*, named after the small dot that would appear when turning off older TV sets, organized TV-turnoff from 1996. The primary activist, US-born David Burke, initiated his crusade by climbing on top of a symbolically busted TV set outside Westminster Abbey in 1996 with a sign reading "Get a Life!" He called on Prince Charles to ban TV cameras from his future coronation – whenever that would be. "As the Queen's coronation in 1953 had marked the start of widespread television viewing in the UK, a TV-free Charles coronation would, felt Burke, have a pleasing symmetry to it" (White dot 2009).

White dot did not believe that television could be improved, but were "against the activity of viewing" (White dot 2000a). The network ran small-scale community events, so-called Zocalos, the Mexican word for town square. Neighbourhoods were leafleted to persuade residents to sit outside their houses for a night instead of watching television (White dot 2000b). *White dot* produced a 300-page resistance manual *Get A Life!* (Burke and Lotus 1998), promoted child-rearing methods from the pre-TV age, and marketed anti-television merchandise, such as TV-B-Gone, a device used to turn off TV-sets in cafes and pubs. Its fundamentalist stance is perhaps most visible in an advert for jewellery made by televisions smashed by the Taliban in Afghanistan, where admiration is expressed for the swift and brutal action:

> You've got to have a sneaking respect for the Taliban. No messing about with posters or TV-B-Gone's for them. They just came into power, outlawed television and rumour has it they publicly executed one just to drive home the point (Adams n.a.).

White dot also speaks out against teaching media literacy and media studies; which "reinforces in students the idea that the spectacle of television should be the centre of their lives":

> It is not in the interest of any media studies professor or textbook author to arrive at the relatively simple truth that maybe television is just not worth the

time. If the "off" button is the answer, then no media studies course will ever help students find it. By ignoring the "off" button, all media studies can only chase its tail (White dot 2000a).

In 2000s, white dot activists authored *Spy TV* (Burke and Lotus 2000), a comprehensive analysis of how digital television collects and sells surveillance data. *Spy TV* suggests that you "visit a department store that sells digital televisions and say you want one that does not offer interactivity, because you have heard they are designed to monitor and manipulate viewers" (141). The authors further invite you to become "Early Rejector" (141), a pun on the concept of "early adopter" from diffusion theory (Rogers 1995). In April 2012, *White dot* tried to use analogue switch-off to get rid of television for good: "When your set goes fuzzy on Wednesday the 4th, don't fiddle with the remote. Throw it away. Mail it to a friend in another country. Get out of the box!" (Burke 2012).

TELEVISION GOES FUZZY

Television turnoff-week reported impressive participation: One million in 1995 (Baker 1996), rising to 7.6 million on the tenth anniversary in 2004 (Cai 2014). Compiling the numbers, it was claimed in 2002 that more than 24 million had participated altogether (TV Turnoff 2002a), rising to over 100 million in 2013 and over 300 million in 2016 (the two last figures are from Wikipedia's and include screen-free week, see Ch. 5 and below). The numbers were based on loose report-backs and sales of turnoff kits, and are in no sense verified. It was also evident that despite all this activism, television was still there. Los Angeles Times even comments on how during the 1996 turnoff, television ratings increased (Dundjerski 1997).

This was not a movement prone to hopelessness, however. "I think any major social movement starts that way," says Labalme in a 1998 interview, staking his hopes on declining standards and increased dissatisfaction: "I hear this more and more from people,... 'I used to watch a lot, but now it's so bad'." Echoing Postman he asserts "As far as we're concerned, the worse the content gets, the greater the likelihood that people will turn away entirely" (Hirsch 1998).

TV-turnoffs continued in the new millennium, but there is change in the air. In 2010, *TV-turnoff week* was changed to *Screen-Free Week*, and, allegedly "at Henry and Matt's request," the site was relocated to the lobby group Campaign for a Commercial-Free Childhood (Screen-free week 2014), a group that does not appear to share the staunch anti-TV-beliefs of *TV-Free America*.

White dot, for its part, continues to update its website with small victories and disappointments. In 2015 they are satisfied that the Catholic Church had got its first TV-free Pope in almost a century, citing Pope Francis as saying that "he promised the Virgin Mary in 1990 that he would never watch again." When the professed non-watcher Ed Miliband became leader of the British Labour Party, the website is hopeful that Britain would get its first TV-free prime minster. As the Conservatives won the 2015 election, the site notes disappointedly "Britain ignores white dot endorsement!" (White dot 2015).

What is at Stake and What to Do?

The traditional positions elaborated in media resistance: that media do not inspire a virtuous life and do not ascribe to the highest cultural standards, inspired plenty of criticism against television. Whitehouse and her campaign is only one of many examples of moral mobilization against what many saw to be a medium spearheading a liberal revolution. The commercial nature of (particularly) US television, the proliferation of violent entertainment, the head-to-head competition between networks driving out material not intended to entertain, provided plenty of fodder for those who saw television as a cause of moral and cultural decline. The values at stake were similar to those that had motivated reactions to novels, serial literature, cinema and comics, but the position of these concerns in society had changed in the television network era. The liberalization of the cultural climate from the 1960s allowed for a wider interpretation of right and wrong in terms of moral behaviour, and a new understanding of cultural value, where also works of popular culture were admired for their quality. As Menand (2011, xxi) puts it, out went the notion that "the fate of the republic is somehow at stake" in the matter of "what kind of art people enjoy or admire."

Other concerns intensified with television, particularly the concern for educational standards, enlightenment and learning. The concern for passive rather than active uses of the mind was a recurring theme; the flow character and the way audiences were seen to become "couch potatoes" were deemed to impair concentration and focus. Passivity was seen as leading to both mental and physical health problems; television viewing was likened to drug use and escalating obesity. Resistance to television was also inspired by its presumed negative effect on involvement in small and large communities – from families to neighbourhoods to municipalities and nations – predating the concerns later spelled out by Robert Putnham in the well-known *Bowling alone* (2000). Television was not social glue, protesters claimed, but a force of fragmentation, leading to a decline in civil engagement.

Resistance to television was motivated by a concern for democracy and political processes. Mander predicted that television would lead to authoritarian rule, while Postman lamented that politics turned into entertainment. Both referred to Orwell and Huxley's dystopic accounts, while TV-turnoff week cited Bradbury to indicate that non-viewers were smarter than viewers. We see how dystopian narratives inspire writers; not directly in the sense that predictions are seen to be true, but as a points of reference and a common vocabulary that can be used to distinguish between and add force to arguments. However, with increasing use of television in western democracies, speculations that television would contribute to all-out dystopia (Chs. 2 and 3) became less prominent. Writers and movements instead used television to explain social ills within existing society.

While different writers and movements ground their resistance in different values, their eclecticism is also striking. The main finding regarding *What is at stake?* is that works of resistance tended to see television's presence and position in society as bad in many different ways. The books and testimonies discussed here are not academic accounts that easily can be placed within a specific theory or position in media studies – such as moral panic or technological determinism – rather they can be read at sense-making efforts reflecting broadly on negative experiences and disappointments (see Sundet 2012). Studies of people who live without television point to a similar diversity. For example, Krcmar's study (2009) shows that people give up television for many different, and often overlapping, reasons; they might be dissatisfied with content, the medium or the industry, and resistance appeals to a diverse mix with different political and religious beliefs. Whereas Krcmar finds no clear pattern in terms of religious or political affiliations, her comparison between viewers and non-viewers point to a higher level of intensity and lower level of pragmatism among non-viewers. The TV-free had noticeably strong opinions, as Krcmar states: "This is a zealous lot" (42).

Protesters against early mass media often campaigned for tighter regulation, and for Whitehouse and others resisting television on moral grounds, this was the right course. For those who saw television to be irredeemable, it was more difficult. Collective action against television was inspired by the writings of Postman, Mander and others, but most importantly by the practical approach of Winn who advocated bottom-up television boycotts. The dominant professions in resistance activities were educational and medical, followed by religious, government/community and sports/outdoors. The strength of the endorsers in the US illustrates the ambivalence and scepticism that many professionals felt towards television; television was widely experienced as invasive, threatening authority and autonomy in fields such as politics, science and education (see also Bourdieu 1998). By endorsing turnoff, organizations and professions could act on their scepticism, and, at the same time, promote their aims and goals to a wider public.

The campaigns shows great flexibility and reflexivity; activists are determined not to come across as moralists or luddites, but as intelligent fun-lovers with better things to do than staring at a screen. Although activities such as *TV-turnoff week* were not immediately effective, abstaining from television could serve a marker of identity. "We do not watch television and in many ways, that is who we are. I think this is a very big thing that defines us," says one of the informants in Krcmar's study (2009, 43). Those who had given up television felt that they "are not giving up anything at all. They are merely living without television to improve their lives" (43). Yet, the study shows, those who did not have television often felt labelled as Luddites or cultural reactionaries. One respondent, who voiced his resistance in Christian terms, said that his peers "think we're in a cult" (58). Another said that the assumption was that non-viewers should "drive a horse and buggy or dress all in black" (59).

One aim of the book is to discuss how resistance is sustained and how arguments and values transcend national, historical and media boundaries. An explanation beginning to emerge is the flexible ideology and adaptable forms of action. Television resistance, as discussed in this chapter, appealed to different segments and different organizational concerns, and could be tailored to fit different national debates. I have shown how resistance travelled, how messages were adjusted, and how turnoffs could be utilized to aid different causes in societies with widely different television systems.

The analysis in this chapter stops in the early 2000s, an era of debate on *The End of Television?* (Katz and Scannell 2009). Anti-television activism did not undermine television, but is an indication of how the medium was contested. The dislike of television became even more visible at the onset of the digital age.

Open Access This chapter is licensed under the terms of the Creative Commons Attribution 4.0 International License (http://creativecommons.org/licenses/by/4.0/), which permits use, sharing, adaptation, distribution and reproduction in any medium or format, as long as you give appropriate credit to the original author(s) and the source, provide a link to the Creative Commons license and indicate if changes were made.

The images or other third party material in this chapter are included in the book's Creative Commons license, unless indicated otherwise in a credit line to the material. If material is not included in the book's Creative Commons license and your intended use is not permitted by statutory regulation or exceeds the permitted use, you will need to obtain permission directly from the copyright holder.

CHAPTER 5

"Caught in the Net": Online and Social Media Disappointment and Detox

Abstract Internet was eagerly awaited as a liberation from television. Yet, a decade into the new century, warnings about the negative consequences of online and social media proliferated. Critics claim that social and online media undermine broadly shared values: morality, culture, enlightenment, democracy, community and health. With increasingly ubiquitous media, the chapter argues that it is difficult to propose political measures to restrict media. However, a parallel development is the emergence of self-help guides, websites and confessionals inspiring users to media detox and abstention.

Keywords Media detox · Self-help · Screen-free · Social media · Online media

A MEDIUM OF TRUTH

Internet brought hope to those who loathed television. In *Life After Television* (1992) US economist and investor George Gilder praised "the teleputer" which would have none of the vulgar properties of television, but greatly enhance democracy and community. Television, in contrast was "a tool of tyrants":

> Its overthrow will be a major force for freedom and individuality, culture and morality. That overthrow is at hand (49).

---

*is used throughout the book to indicate my translation.

Negroponte (1995), Rheingold (1993), Turkle (1995) and others predicted that digitalization would bring human liberation, a genuine public sphere and more creative management of identity. Al Gore, US Vice President from 1993 to 2001, was also a cyber-optimist who in office initiated crucial legislation for expanding the Internet. Gore blamed television for "hollowing-out" American democracy (10), whereas Internet was "perhaps the greatest source of hope":

> An important distinction to make is that the Internet is not just another platform for disseminating the truth. It's a platform for *pursuing* the truth, and the decentralized creation and distribution of ideas... It's a platform, in other words, for reason (2007, 260).

Not since radio had a media technology been met with such praise for its inherently positive properties (Ch. 2). But not all were convinced. Voices of warning sounded: the Internet could be even worse than television! As Kimberly Young puts it in her 1998 bestseller *Caught in the Net* (13),

> Rather than becoming the technological savior of our time, the Internet just might be emerging as the addiction of the millennium, surpassing even TV with its pervasive grip on our minds and souls.

Other warnings targeted the cumulative effects of too many media. "This book originates from an acute feeling that something is about to go wrong," Norwegian anthropologist Thomas Hylland Eriksen started the preface of his bestseller *Tyranny of the moment: fast and slow time in the information age** (2001). Eriksen saw online communication as yet another interruption technology undermining concentration and focus. Echoing warnings against print, early mass media and broadcasting (Chs. 2–4) Eriksen claims that we "are in the process of becoming enslaved by the technology that was supposed to liberate us." Although we have access to more information than before, we are not "better informed" but rather "more confused"* (7).

In this chapter the emphasis is neither predominantly on resistance to new media (Chs. 2 and 3), nor predominantly on mature media (Ch. 4), but on how resistance develops and changes as digital media evolve. The chapter discusses what was at stake for resisters: How were online and social media seen to undermine broadly shared values, and what were the proposed forms of action? The chapter begins with a discussion of writers and books; a selection of non-fiction bestsellers identifying the Internet, online and social media as a cause of social change to the worse. I present the arguments of writers such as Kimberly Young, Andrew Keen, Nicholas Carr, and Sherry Turkle and relate these to the previously identified concerns for morality, culture, enlightenment, democracy, community and health. From resistance literature, I turn to resistance activities, and predominantly the trend towards media abstention, fasting and detox. Although there are still demands for regulation and restrictions, there is widespread acceptance that social and online media are here to stay, and that one can only handle the negative implications through the twin methods of conversation and self-regulation: controlling consumption and talking about the problems in the public sphere. Also in this chapter, most of the cases and examples are from the US, supplemented with European and Scandinavian examples. With social and online media as global entities, I find no sharp distinction between the type of resistance emerging in the US and Europe; the same forms of activism prevail across borders.

In the previous chapter I distinguished between those who believed that television could be improved and those preferring it to be abolished, but a similar distinction is difficult to draw with online and social media. First, it is more difficult to separate between good and bad aspects of online media as a multitude of devices, products, services and genres are intertwined and interlinked (Creeber and Martin 2009). Resistance is also harder to pinpoint because writers and activists are increasingly self-reflexive and keenly aware of the social stigma of being "against" media and technology. There is much strong polemic against online and social media, but writers still go to great lengths to tell readers that they are not against the detested entities. For example, Andrew Keen, author of *The Cult of the Amateur*, a bestseller with the strong and explicit subtitle: *How the Internet is Killing Our Culture* (2007), turns out not to be against the murdering force after all. In one of several disclaimers, he writes the following:

> I am neither antitechnology nor antiprogress. Digital technology is a miraculous thing, giving us the means to globally connect and share knowledge in unprecedented ways. This book certainly couldn't have been completed without e-mail or the Internet, and I'm the last person

to romanticize a past in which we wrote letters by candlelight and had them delivered by Pony Express (184–185).

With online media, many actors voicing concerns are themselves Internet savvy: media professionals, innovators and "techies" who are disappointed with outcome of the digital revolution. These transformations make for an interesting discussion of the status of media resistance in the twenty-first century. In one sense, we are all partly or sometimes resisters trying to avoid invasive services and restrict the role played by ubiquitous media in our lives (see also Karlsen and Syvertsen 2016; Portwood-Stacer 2012). In another sense, there are very few resisters, as few of those voicing dire predictions set out concrete proposals for change.

Heroin in School Milk

Internet's history can be traced back to the first computers of the 1940s and attempts to connect computers to each other from the 1960s (Hannemyr 1999, 12–15). In the 1990s, hypertext and World Wide Web became the "killer application" for Internet's growth into a mainstream media platform (Liestøl 1999, 542). The 1990s was a decade of cyber-optimism, but amidst enthusiasm were public concerns for morality, sexual and violent content (Karlsen 2013). Concerns were raised that children would "fall prey to child molesters hanging out in electronic chat rooms," a phrase used in a cover story in Time Magazine July 1995 (cited from Sutter 2003, 170). The dangers of the Internet inspired new and revitalized metaphors in media resistance. Frank Cook, a British member of Parliament in 1994 described computer pornography as "tantamount to the injection of heroin into a child's school milk" (cited from Sutter 2003, 170). Video games were called "murder simulators" (Vitka 2005). Regulation was initiated, such as the amendments in the US *Communications Decency Act of 1996* to protect minors against online pornography (Brisbin 2004, 6) and ratings systems to warn against violent games (Ferguson 2013, 27).

One of the writers who best seized the early concerns was Kimberly Young, in two books with the metaphorical titles *Caught in the net* (1998) and *Tangled in the Web* (2000). Young, a clinical psychologist, warns that Internet might have "harmful consequences that, left undetected and unchecked, could silently run rampant in our schools, our universities, our offices, our libraries, and our homes" (1998, 11). If you hook your children up with modems,

> you may unwittingly be opening the door to marathon chat sessions that lead to declining grades, secret plots to run away with cyberfriend, and a disconnection of family life more destructive than stationing individual TV sets in every room of the house (28).

Young realized she had "hit a nerve" when journalists began to swarm around her at conferences and her observations were reported across the globe (1998, 5–6). What is at stake for Young is mental and physical health: Internet is addictive and Young soon established her own treatment programme inspired by Alcoholics Anonymous (Young 1998, 109). In addition to health, morality and community was also at stake; her books are full of stories of law-abiding citizens spiralling into destruction. A typical story in *Tangled in the web* begins like this: "John is a forty-three-year-old engineer living in Maine who considered himself a devote Christian and a good family man." Trouble begins when the family buys a computer "for the boys' education and for John to update the household finances." Two pages into the story John has lost his job and his marriage, and the FBI takes him away in handcuffs for trading in child pornography (2000, 29–31).

Generically, Young's books resemble those of Marie Winn who wrote critically about television, both are filled with testimonials and practical advice (Ch. 4). And Winn herself joined the chorus of concern, updating her arguments about negative effects of media. In a 25th anniversary of *The Plug-in-Drug*, subtitled *Television, Computers, And Family Life* (2002) she warns that computers are just as bad as television, they are "hypnotic and addictive" (195), and may lead to more violence and extremism (166). Winn is particularly critical of the teaching profession for diluting its media-critical stance; while teachers saw television "as a *cause* of certain problems" in the 1970s, a new generation, tended to see computers "as a potential *cure* for those same problems," she notes disappointedly (174).

While teachers were getting enthusiastic, others were getting disappointed. As digital media evolved, writers from other professions, among them media people, "techies" and innovators, began to resist. In international bestsellers published in 2008, 2010 and 2011, Keen, Carr and Turkle describe how the digital revolution is turning society in the wrong direction.

Orwell and Huxley Were Wrong! Keen and the Loss of Culture

British-born media entrepreneur Andrew Keen describes himself as "a classic example of the immigrant entrepreneur who came to America seeking more economic and cultural freedom" (2008, 37). In 1995 he founded Audiocafe.com, a first generation Internet company. In a 2007 bestseller, *The Cult of the Amateur: How the Internet is Killing Our Culture*, Keen describes how he "peddled the original Internet dream," he "seduced investors" and "almost became rich." But sometime in 2004, with the emergence of participatory and personalized services, the dream turned sour. Keen was present at an event organized by the O'Reilly consultancy, key ideologue of Web 2.0, where "democratization" was on everyone's lips (Keen 2008, 11–15, see also O'Reilly 2011). But instead Keen became convinced that services such as *Wikipedia, MySpace* and *Youtube* would be "undermining truth, souring civic discourse, and belittling expertise, experience and talent" (15). He says of his conversion:

> This, therefore, is no ordinary critique of Silicon Valley. It's the work of an apostate, and insider now on the outside who has poured out his cup of Kool-Aid and resigned his membership in the cult (11–12).

Keen's is a classic dystopic tale; Huxley, Bradbury and Orwell are all points of reference in his work (Keen 2008, 2011). But neither of them got the destructive elements exactly right, mostly because they did not foresee the influx of ordinary people into the production circuit. The danger was not an authoritarian state and *The Cult of the Amateur* is not "Brave New World 2.0" as suggested by an acquaintance; instead the technological shift was bringing us "an endless digital forest of mediocrity" (Keen 2008, 2–3).

To Keen, almost everything is at stake. Social and online media destroy morality by encouraging piracy and gambling, narcissism and pornography. Health is at stake as Internet is "altering the shape and chemistry of our brains" and we can expect more "mental disorders such as autism, attention deficit disorder, and hyperactivity" (163). Democracy is undermined by bloggers using "digital media to obfuscate truth and manipulate public opinion" (26). Enlightenment is threatened: where utopians see the overthrow of "dictatorship of expertise," Keen sees the emergence of "dictatorship of idiots" (35). Above all, what is at stake is culture. Keen admits to being "an elitist" (2008, xiii), but defends Bob Dylan as much as classical music, network television as much as classical literature. Culture is, what is being produced by professionals, by cultural and media institutions, now "under assault" (7). His comments on television are respectful and nostalgic:

> In the golden age of media, revered journalists like Edward R. Murrow and Walter Cronkite were cultural heroes – universally admired, trusted and respected. But in today's word they would be C-list celebrities, as fewer and fewer of us pay attention to the traditional news media (83).

Alluding to Time Magazine making YOU person of the year in 2006, he concludes with a strong appeal "to protect mainstream media against the cult of the amateur" (204):

> So let's not go down in history as that infamous generation who, intoxicated by the ideal of democratization, killed professional mainstream media. Let's not be remembered for replacing movies, music and books with YOU! (204–205)

Web 2.0 launched a whole new round of cyber-optimism (see, for example, Benkler 2006; Lessig 2008; Shirky 2010). But more works of disappointment and resistance were beginning to emerge.

Discourse of Disappointment: Carr and Turkle

As a writer and editor, Nicolas Carr had found Web 2.0 "new and liberating." He became "a social networker and a content generator" (15). But then: "Sometime in 2007, a serpent of doubt slithered into my info-paradise" (16). In yet another enthusiast-turned-sceptic bestseller, *The Shallows: What the internet is doing to our brains*, published in 2010, he observes: "I'm not thinking the way I used to think" (2011, 5–6):

> I feel it most strongly when I'm reading. I used to find it easy to immerse myself in a book or a lengthy article.... That's rarely the case anymore. Now my concentration starts to drift after a page or two.... The deep reading that used to come naturally has become a struggle.

He has the explanation:

> I think I know what's going on. For well over a decade now, I've been spending a lot of time online, searching and surfing and sometimes adding to the great databases of the Internet.

Carr grounds his observations in neuroscience and ideas that the brain is changeable and plastic (27). With electronic media, the pathways in our brains are being "rerouted" (77). We sacrifice mental skills that may be more valuable than the ones we gain (35), and end up with a "juggler's brain" (115). With digital communications, a new mode is beginning to take hold, the mode of shallowness: "It's possible to think deeply while surfing the Net, just as it is possible to think shallowly while reading a book, but that's not the type of thinking the technology encourages and rewards" (115–116).

What is at stake for Carr is enlightenment, in particular concentration, focus and reading. "For the last five centuries, ever since Gutenberg's printing press made book reading a popular pursuit, the linear, literary mind has been at the center of art, science, and society," Carr writes in a sweeping and typical phrase. But now "It may soon be yesterday's mind" (2011, 10). Carr's arguments resembles Neil Postman's critique of television two decades earlier (Ch. 4), but for Carr, previous electric and electronic media are a mere footnote. These media had limited influence because they were "limited by their inability to transmit the written word" (77).

In her 2011 bestseller *Alone together: Why we expect more from technology and less from each other*, Sherry Turkle, writer and professor at MiT, details her digital autobiography; also a journey from hope to scepticism (xiii). She describes how her first book, published in 1984, was hopeful and optimistic on behalf of new technology, in contrast to Orwell's *Nineteen Eighty-four* celebrated that same year (xi). A second book, published in 1995, also offered "a positive view of new opportunities for exploring identity online" (xi). After that however, "my concerns have grown" (xii). The developments that she finds most disturbing have to do with loss of community and erosion of interpersonal bonds. She is concerned about new types of robots, not just developed to do dangerous jobs but also to be friends, pets and lovers. And she is concerned about ubiquity; that we are always logged on. "I feel witness for a third time to a turning point in our expectations of technology and ourselves," she writes, we have come to "expect more from technology and less from each other" (xii).

Turkle notices that people were beginning to prefer "machine-mediated relationships," teenagers would rather text than talk and adults felt that "real time" events were taking too much time (11). In her description of what is lost, she praises non-media activities and older mass media:

> But if you're spending three, four, or five hours a day in an online game or virtual world (a time commitment that is not unusual), there's got to be someplace you're not. And that someplace you're not is often with your family or friends – sitting around, playing Scrabble face-to-face, taking a walk, watching a movie together in the old-fashioned way (12).

Turkle comments on situations where people are "alone together" and observes metaphorically that "[l]ife in a media bubble has come to seem natural" (16).

Turkle's main concern is with social disconnection, but the metaphor of "bubble" is also used to express political concerns. Parisier (2011) warns of "filter bubbles" where personalized algorithms prevent users from being confronted with viewpoints they disagree with, and terms like "echo chamber" and "egocasting" (Rosen 2004) describe similar dangers. Evgeney Morozov, who has written several books about the use of online media by authoritarian regimes, use chapter titles inspired by dystopian fiction, such as "Orwell's Favorite Lolcat" and "The Orwell-Huxley Sandwich has Expired" to discuss modern-day threats to democracy. These terms, metaphors and perspectives pose a potent antidote to cyber-utopian notions of Internet as a platform of reason and truth.

A CALL TO CONVERSE

When Turkle voices her concerns to friends, they shrug and ask "What are you going to do?" (2011, 296). Turkle suggests to begin with simple things such as "Talk to colleagues down the hall, no cell phones at dinner, on the playground, in the car or in company" (296). Although several of her solutions pertain to self-regulation, Turkle warns against framing the problem as "addiction" (293). This would imply that "there is only one solution":

> To combat addiction you have to discard the addicting substance. But we are not going to "get rid" of the Internet. We will not go "cold turkey" or

forbid cell phones to our children. We are not going to stop the music or go back to television as the family hearth (293–294).

Also Young, Winn, Hylland-Eriksen, Keen and Carr declare that they do not wish to get rid of the Internet and are not against online and social media. However, what also unite these writers is the struggle to define a forceful stance; how do you position yourself as a strong critic of online and social media while avoiding to be seen as being against media? It is easy to sympathize with these writers as they get pushed into corners by "the myopia of the digital mob" (Keen 2008, xiv); some are subject to vicious personal attacks, illustrating the difficulty of establishing a media-resistant or technology-resistant position. In long passages in prefaces and postscripts, writers reflect upon the reception of their ideas and express resentment at the labels they are awarded. Despite their forceful language and frequently dystopic predictions, it is interesting to note that most respond to criticism by attempting to place themselves in a centrist position. Carr refers to the continuous debates between "Philistines" vs. "Luddites" (2–3), but position himself outside this dichotomy (Chs. 1 and 4). Keen is irritated that he is called a Luddite (xiv) and describes himself as a "pragmatist" (196). In an afterword to the Paperback Edition, Morozov reflects on the reception of his book and the assumption that he advocates "some kind of cyber-scepticism bordering on cyber-defeatism," claiming that his position rightly is one of "*cyber-agnosticism*" (336–337). However, he concedes that his stance in his first book "was not crystal clear, hence the preponderance of critical interpretations that put me squarely in the dystopian corner."

In addition to difficulties in defining a forceful stance, writers struggle with identifying paths of action. Different ideas and suggestions are aired, including proposals for regulation, but, in general, there does not seem to be much hope in political or legal solutions. Instead, the writers are eager to stimulate public talk and conversation. Early in the book Turkle writes "This is the time to begin these conversations, together" (17) and the concluding chapter is called "Necessary Conversations." Keen states explicitly that he wants to start a "conversation" and encourages readers to "talk about the consequences of today's user-generated media before it is too late" (xiv). Like the others he is encouraged by the response: "I think I have succeeded, both in America and all over the world." Since the book came out (xv):

> I've been fortunate to talk with many thousands of people who, like me, are deeply worried and confused about the economic, cultural, and ethical

consequences of our user-generated media revolution. The digital mob might hate me, but many others – teachers, recording engineers, politicians, musicians, librarians, parents, publishers, graphic artists, intellectual property lawyers, filmmakers, media entrepreneurs, and other professionals – are on my side.

Also Carr is encouraged by various forms of talk and conversation. He tells of loneliness in writing *The Shallows*, it felt like paddling a small and empty boat "against a very strong tide" (225). But the book became a bestseller, letters and emails poured in, other books emerged. He states hopefully: "A backlash against the Net, it seems, is under way" (2011, 225) and "Some kind of rebellion seems in order" (227). However, as to what kind of rebellion, he turns poetic rather than political. The last sentences in the afterword are the following:

> We may be wary of what our devices are doing to us, but we're using them more than ever. And yet, history tells us, it's only against such powerful cultural currents that countercultural movements take shape. As I said, it's a small boat. But there's still plenty of room inside. Feel free to grab an oar (228).

The appeals to start and take part in conversations, instead of setting out long-term political goals, allude to idealistic notions of dialogue in the public sphere (Habermas 1984). Ironically, it is with social and online media that the spaces for public conversations have most expanded in recent decades; there are endless new opportunities for conversation in blogs, podcasts, social media and online forums. With calls for more conversation, social and online media sceptics find themselves in the paradoxical position of having to rely on the objects of dislike, while at the same time arguing that these should play a less important role.

A MEDIA RESISTANCE RALLY

On the 12th of May, 2012, 40,000 Orthodox Jewish men filled a sport stadium in Queens to protest the Internet's damaging influence. Desktops, laptops and smartphones posed new challenges to a community that routinely discouraged television ownership (Fitzpatrick 2012). The demand for tickets at the rally was so high that an extra sports stadium with 20,000 seats was rented. Organizing the event involved "more than 750 buses, a few boats, 28 state agencies" (Stein, 2012). Women could not participate, but could listen to the speeches in Hebrew, English and Yiddish streamed to Orthodox communities around New York (Grynbaum 2012).

Eytan Kobre (2012), a lawyer and spokesperson, describes the motivation for the rally in the New York Post, echoing almost all major concerns in media resistance. One big concern was with morality, "the pervasive accessibility of pornography online, which has reached epidemic proportions," which "debases and objectifies women" and leads to violence. Democracy was at stake as "verbal violence" polluted the societal atmosphere and inflamed aggression. Community was undermined as "we've replaced conversation with tweeting and twittering our way through cyberspace." In a phrase that resonates with centuries of resistance statements, Kobre argued as follows:

> No one lives in the moment anymore. No longer are people able to be alone with themselves and comfortable without being connected to other people. Gadgets are supposed to free us, but ironically, they have enslaved us and left us with much less time for ourselves, our families and the things that are important in life.

Also enlightenment, and particularly education, was undermined; Internet was corrupting the brains of students and there was "no research anymore" and "no retention of information."

The rally was highly unusual in a Western context; invoking memories of demonstrations against early popular media and television (Chs. 2 and 4). But this time there was no political manifesto and no clear demands to regulators and industry. Observers and journalists struggled to make sense of the diverse messages from speakers and participants, was this rally against the Internet or was it "just to make it Kosher," as one of the participants put it (Miller 2012)? Interviews and news reports from the rally show how also an orthodox religious congregation struggled to find means to act on their media resistance.

On one level, the message was one of self-discipline as members of the congregation were urged to install filters against pornography (Miller 2012). But organizers pointed out that more was needed in order to combat the enormous problems caused by new digital media: "It is fully recognized that this is far, far from the conclusive answer to the problems the Internet poses – it is merely a first step evidencing our seriousness and resolve to find the best solutions and implement them." But what would be the second step? Seemingly at loss for a more potent medicine, organizers proposed more of the same – more meetings and conversations. The next step would be gatherings around the country "reaching out to other faiths – and society as a whole" (Kobre 2012).

SELF-HELP AND DETOX

Parallel to the emergence of literature pointing to negative consequences of social and online media in society, there has been a proliferation of talk and conversation about personal forms of regulation and abstention. Media self-help tips are available on many platforms: in media reports, social media, websites, and books with titles such as *Unfriend Yourself: Three days to Discern, Detox and Decide about Social Media* (Tennant 2012; see also, among others, Green 2014; Zane 2014). The values and concerns expressed in these texts echo the general concerns in media resistance, and advice is given as to how one can become a more authentic human being and lead a more valuable life by restricting media engagement.

In media policy studies, the term self-regulation describes the trend whereby media companies increasingly regulate themselves, rather than being regulated by the state (Campbell 1999). However, the term can also describe the development whereby users increasingly have to self-regulate their behaviour so media do not become too invasive. Typically media self-help guides begins by recommending that the user assess the situation and make a plan, before implementing a programme for management of time, space and identity (see Karlsen and Syvertsen 2016). Time-management is often the most important remedy, for example, the self-help book: *Get the F*ck out of Social Media*, Green (2014) suggests:

> Instead of totally removing yourself from the internet, try to gradually reduce the time spent online. Start with 20 minutes. The increase to 30, then 45, then an hour or so on...(sic) Strike the right balance between chatting, playing, commenting etc. (How to overcome Social Media Addiction, para 1.)

The advice is strikingly similar to advice regarding smoking, drinking, overeating and other ills, and more detailed advice follow. Users are told to turn off notifications, remove apps and services, and physically remove screens from sight. Self-help guides also encourage users to instigate deeper life changes to distance themselves from the constant interruptions, narcissism and procrastination encouraged by social and online media. Common advice in media self-help guides reflect concerns for morality (avoid pornography and cybersex), community (spend more time with others, volunteer), democracy (be active in social movements, engage in politics), health (be outdoors and do more exercise) and enlightenment (switch to more learned pastimes). A particularly strong recommendation is to switch electric and electronic media for print, as in *How to Reclaim Your Life from Facebook* (Zane 2014, ch. 6, para 5):

> Consider joining a book club where you will get out, meet new people and broaden your knowledge on available literature or specific topics... Reading is also part of educating ourselves and improving our knowledge of any topic, work or professional, hobby or artistic endeavour. Consider reading an opportunity to discover more about the world, about yourself and your fellow citizens.

A change away from a strong media identity will presumably increase your happiness and refocus your attention on what is more important, realizing that "Life is so much more than pixels, bites and likes" (Bratsberg and Moen 2015, 17*) (see also Chs. 4 and 6).

Connected with self-help advice, testimonials and confessionals where individuals share experiences with media detox and abstention in the public sphere have also proliferated. The testimonies reflect the increasingly porous distinction between popular science and journalism on the one hand, and the relaying of personal experiences on the other, and is part of the influx of self-therapeutic discourse into the public sphere (Madsen 2010, 2014; Illouz 2008). Media detox accounts are published in all formats and involve anything from the strictest to the mildest measures. Blogs and posts on social media describe measures such as "Facebook suicide" and tell how you can "Destroy your carefully constructed virtual image in four easy clicks" (King 2008). Bratsberg and Moen (2015) tells of a digital business developer who chose a meditation retreat in India for her digital detox; she was totally removed from human contact in ten days to learn to be "more present in the moment" (42–43). Some do not aim to quit but go for an extended fast. In *The Verge*, technology writer Paul Miller (2013) explains how he came to do a one-year detox:

In early 2012 I was 26 years old and burnt out. I wanted a break from modern life – the hamster wheel of an email inbox, the constant flood of WWW information which drowned out my sanity. I wanted to escape.

The media detox confessional is also found in book-length accounts. In *The Winter of Our Disconnect: How Three Totally Wired Teenagers (and a Mother Who Slept with Her iPhone) Pulled the Plug on Their Technology and Lived to Tell the Tale* (2010), Susan Maushart reports on her family's six months media fast. Maushart, a journalist holding a PhD from New York University and dedicating the book to television resister Neil Postman (see Ch. 4), writes in capacity of parent. "Over a period of years," she writes, "I watched and worried as our media began to function as a force field separating my children from what my son, only half ironically, called RL (Real Life)" (1–2). She observes that the more family members communicated individually, the less they cohered as a family (6), illustrating the concerns of Turkle and others (above). The family's detox is successful and life changing: the son discovers a hidden musical talent, the youngest daughter begins to sleep regularly and her moodiness improves, the family finds energy for activities such as playing games, reading and cooking, they bond and reconnect. In another book-length report Lars Bratsberg, who works for Google in Norway, reports similar benefits after sixteen days of detox in order to normalize his online media use (Bratsberg and Moen 2015).

Not just family life, also work life is reported to benefit from detox. Agnes Ravatn is a Norwegian acclaimed author, who used six years to write a second novel, due to online procrastination. "Day after day, year after year, I had to realize that I had done nothing else than being on internet and mobile, caught in vastness," she writes in *Operation self-discipline** (2014) – described as a "self-help book for those who hate self-help books."* A combination of strict self-regulation and writing about the experience massively improved her life:

> Throughout the short year I have worked with this book, my everyday life has indeed been substantially changed to the better, primarily in the area that revolves around work. I will almost say it so strongly that I have been born-again, work wise. Primarily because I finally to a large extent managed to free myself from online newspapers, email checking, and the smartphone. I have simply become an extremist when it comes to internet (86).*

Self-help is often seen as a form of narcissistic self-obsession, but as pointed out by McGee (2005), it can more adequately be seen as a necessary form of labour. In an era of deregulation and increasingly conflicting impulses, you cannot expect others to solve your problems, rather there is cultural accept for expecting you to get a grip (Madsen 2010, 87). Illouz (2008, 243) points out that therapy and self-help works because it offers tools and technologies to manage problems in a complex culture "riddled with contradictory normative imperatives." And with social and online media you cannot really blame the platforms; as you – yourself – are part of the problem. Much self-help literature makes an effort to shift responsibility from media operators to users, as in Tennant (2012):

> When I say, "Facebook tells us lies" or "Facebook makes us promises it doesn't keep", I do not mean Facebook the corporation. I mean Facebook the website and the culture we have created around it. More often than not, Facebook allows us to make these promises, and we propagate them (Don't be a hater, para 4).

While self-help books and confessionals insist that something must be done, they take care not to moralize. It is not a case of us versus you, as Bratsberg and Moen (2015, 17) insists, we are all in the same boat:

> This book is not intended to be a nagging-book [kjeftebok] where we talk about how stupid you are, if you never put away the phone or look up from the screen…We've been there, yes, we are there still to some extent.*

"I'M UNPLUGGING FOR #SCREENFREEWK"

In the previous chapter, I described how organizations such as *White dot* and *TV-Free America* organized short-term TV-boycott in schools, communities and homes. Although many participants may not have agreed, the political goal was to get rid of television (Ch. 4). In the 2000s, *TV-turnoff Week* changed its focus to *Digital Detox Week* or *Screen-Free Week* in many countries, reflecting the proliferation of new media. With the name change came also a political reorientation, as the screen free-movement appeared to sever the link between short-term boycotts and long-term elimination.

In Norway, the Christian media watch organization Family and Media organizes screen-free weeks and describe their ideology on the website (Familie og medier 2012):

> There is no doubt: The screens are here to stay. And, as many will agree, that is a good thing. Whether it is at home or at work, there is much benefit and enjoyment in the many media channels. But, as with anything useful and fun, the many screens can get a larger space in everyday life than they deserve. Every year, during Lent, we encourage in you to take a week off from all screens. Turn off and see what happens!*

The US campaign has a similar focus; emphasizing that you can still use devices for work or school, but should try to avoid digital entertainment and screens interfering with family time and meals (Screen-Free Week 2016b).

The disclaimers are familiar from resistance literature: online services are here to stay, and although excessive screen time may be bad for you and your family, elimination is no goal. However, the methods and advice recommended by the screen-free movement also reflect the increasing difficulties with practicing media resistance in the age of ubiquity. A particular problem is how to decide what services to abstain from and which to keep when you are doing media detox. While a television turnoff only required pushing a button, the most ardent also refusing to appear on television to propagate their case, no such limitations exists for the screen-free. Indeed, if you follow on-site advice, you can end up spending a lot of time online, as screen activities are recommended throughout the process of detox, from preparation to debrief.

In the media detox planning phase you are pointed to many sites where you can assess your situation. You can for example take an online test with questions such as *How often do you find that you stay online longer than originally intended?* to find out how big your problem is (Center for Internet Addiction 2009). Several sites also recommend or offer the possibility of testing whether you are able to sit still and stare at a screen for a designed period without touching a keyboard. *Adbusters* digital detox week-preparations begins with the suggestion that you take a "Zen moment": sixty seconds of staring at the dark screen and "[m]editate about your relationship with the box"

(Adbusters 2015), whereas Bratsberg and Moen (2015) recommend a website where you can check if you manage to stare at the screen and listen to the sound of waves for two full minutes.

Once you have finished screen staring and decided to go offline, there is more online work to do. A Norwegian newspaper describes the efforts of a student who takes part in screen-free week and her struggle to separate acceptable and non-acceptable use (No: downloading music from the Internet, Yes: listen to music already downloaded). She has a long list of chores to do before starting, including "tell people that I'm not available on Facebook so that they can submit necessary information by phone" (Hamerstad and Almelid 2012). During the actual detox there is also a lot of online activity. You can get constant updates on Facebook, you can add your event to an online map and become an endorser for that year's week online, you can download the turn-off kit and sign an online pledge where you specify what screen-free week means in your case. You are also encouraged to use social media to mobilize:

> Spread the Word: Whether you blog, reach out to your local paper, or post to your Facebook page, make sure to let people know you're going screen-free. You'll inspire others, start important conversations, and shine a much-needed spotlight on the importance of carving out screen-free time for children. Here are a few sample posts and tweets, and a sample press release to help you get started (2016a).

Sample tweets include "I'm unplugging for #ScreenFreeWk." "[T]turn off screens and turn on life!" "We're going screen-free. You can too!". "Celebrate #ScreenFreeWk."

Once you are done with the detox it is time to plan for long-term changes, a phase which also require online activity, such as downloading tips to screen-proof your home. Finally, you can buy online apps and filters to help you regulate you relationship with media long-term. For example, the app "Freedom" from *Block digital distractions* is marketed with the texts: "If online distractions kill your productivity, Freedom could be the best 10 dollars you'll ever spend."

A spokesperson for Family and Media, the Norwegian screen-free coordinator, said in 2006: "This is not a media protest, but a campaign to place the media in a richer perspective" (Mz 2006). From a protest against media, it seems, media turnoff has become, in many instances, just another media activity.

What is at Stake and What to do?

Historical conditions and social forces shape media resistance, and resistance to social and online media differs from both television resistance and resistance to early mass media. Although arguments continue to be value-based, specific concerns and actions differ, reflecting changes in media and society. The chapter shows that moral considerations remain a motive for resisting media; and that sexual content, pornography and violence, as well as narcissism in social media, continues to prompt disbelief and dismay. However, it is interesting to note how moral resistance not necessarily entails an expectation or a demand that the offending content will be restricted and curtailed. The situation reflects the massive changes in media regulation and the overall regulatory context; with the liberalization of media and telecom since the 1990s, many media-critical organizations have shifted attention from regulation to raising awareness (Reading 1999, 175) and campaigners instead lobby for technologies that individuals and households can use to censor themselves (Heins 2007; Guins 2009).

The concern that media destroy culture is also expressed differently with social and online media. While the concern in the early era of mass media was to protect high culture and genuine folk culture, it is increasingly popular culture and the cultural industries that are seen to be threatened. In an era where anyone can produce and distribute cultural products, mainstream mass media culture is defended against the "endless digital forest of mediocrity" (Keen 2008). Particularly interesting is how some critics point to television as a professional and unifying medium in the public sphere, representing higher quality as well as an alternative to the isolating "bubbles" created by social and online media (see also Enli et al. 2013). Established mass media are perceived as means to combat fragmentation and sustaining community, as well as sustaining a level of professionalism and quality in cultural production.

Many writers began as digital enthusiasts, but changed their minds due to negative experiences. More than anything, the sentiments emerging are not panic and fear, but disappointment and distrust. Disappointment is particularly linked with two aspects: that digital media did not improve learning and enlightenment, and did not improve democracy. Digital media are potentially great vehicles for learning, but also vehicles for distraction and procrastination. At the height of the television era, there was great concern for passivity and people becoming "couch potatoes," while the most prevalent concerns today is with loss of linearity and a form of hyperactivity, resulting in a "jugglers brain" (Carr 2011). Maybe the strongest assertion made by cyber-enthusiasts was that digital media would enhance democracy; however, Internet did not turn out to be a medium of truth, but could also be used for propaganda and to empower authoritarian regimes. A range of examples, ranging from online surveillance and the emergence of "fake news", to the failure of much hyped "social media revolutions" in the Middle East, punctured hope that online media would improve democratic conditions.

In the previous chapter (Ch. 4), I distinguished between those who believed that television could be improved and those who saw it as irredeemable, and showed how the anti-television movement chose boycotts as one method to get rid of television. Generically, the literature discussed in this chapter shows great similarities to texts discussed previously; writers issue warnings, cite dystopian fiction, use sweeping statements and strong metaphors, point to Internet and digital media as sources of social change to the worse, impose a sense of urgency and use words like "rebellion" – which should indicate that change was imperative. Although many societal problems are identified, few political solutions are advocated. The writers are highly self-reflexive, and use much space to refute criticism that they are moralists, laggards or luddites. Some still advocate regulation, but the main approach is a combination of self-regulation and starting a conversation. As politics and technologies change, acts and expressions of media resistance may be found in everyday media management and the sharing of experiences.

In this chapter, I have pointed to a proliferation of texts advocating media self-help, detox and fasting. Denial of foodstuffs and self-control is a familiar theme in the modern world; media fasting and detox reflect yet another way for individuals to handle the contradictions of modernity (Giddens 1991; Illouz 2008). With media detox, media resistance has developed its own brand of asceticism, as self-discipline, self-denial and self-restraint are means to achieve media resistance goals (see Adair-Toteff 2015). In contrast to religious fasting, which is meant to bring the subjects closer to God, media fasting, even when advocated by religious groups, appear to be more about becoming a more authentic person. Yet, it is interesting to observe how churches and religious groups manage to blend centuries-old practices with modern media resistance, moving seamlessly from "fasting" to "media fasting", illuminating again the flexibility of the cause. In addition to improving your lifestyle and authenticity, media abstention can be used to communicate to others that you are a unique and disciplined human being. Media abstention may function as a marker of identity; a form of "conspicous non-consumption," a term derived from the concept of "conspicuous consumption" whereby the leisure class put their wealth on display (Portwood-Stacer 2012).

With the fragmentation and proliferation of resistance, it is difficult to identify specific professions that are more active than others in online and social media resistance, and it is also difficult to identify differences in concerns and methods across national borders. What I have shown as a general characteristic is that many of those protesting are media savvy. Resistance is no longer a clear-cut case of "us" and "them": of "us" convincing "them" not to use bad media, now resistance, as well as acceptance, is to some extent part of everyone's toolbox. In an era of ubiquitous media, we all need a measure of resistance, or at least a strategy for self-regulation, to prevent media from being too invasive.

Open Access This chapter is licensed under the terms of the Creative Commons Attribution 4.0 International License (http://creativecommons.org/licenses/by/4.0/), which permits use, sharing, adaptation, distribution and reproduction in any medium or format, as long as you give appropriate credit to the original author(s) and the source, provide a link to the Creative Commons license and indicate if changes were made.

The images or other third party material in this chapter are included in the book's Creative Commons license, unless indicated otherwise in a credit line to the material. If material is not included in the book's Creative Commons license and your intended use is not permitted by statutory regulation or exceeds the permitted use, you will need to obtain permission directly from the copyright

CHAPTER 6

What if Resisters were Right? Speculations about Bad Media in Popular Films

Abstract Media resistance is a recurring theme in contemporary culture, and inspire fiction writers as well as film-makers. This chapter discusses dystopian films where media are portrayed as evil, dangerous or bad in other ways. *Being there* (1979), *Videodrome* (1983), *The Truman Show* (1998), *Disconnect* (2012) and *Her* (2013) reflect criticism of network television, video and cable, reality television, social and online media, and virtual reality. The films aid the discussion in the book by providing speculative answers to the question: What if resisters were right? What would our world look like if their warnings came true?

Keywords Films about media · Dystopian films · Science fiction films · Invasive media

DOOMSDAY WITH A LOWER-CASE D

The relationship between media and media resistance is complicated and multifaceted. On the one hand, many journalistic pieces have been based on evidence and arguments collected by media-critical activists mobilizing for control and restrictions, and media resisters have frequently been invited to debates and talk shows to argue their case. On the other hand, media protesters and sceptics have been welcome objects of critique, satire and ridicule, and have often felt that the odds were stacked against them in media coverage (see, for example, Whitehouse 1993, 168; Barker 1984a, 57; Postman 2005b, xvi; Mander 1978, 341–343). The unescapable reciprocity between media and resisters – and the oscillation between a sympathetic and unsympathetic portrayal of media criticism and resistance – is visible not only in factual genres, but also in fiction and entertainment. In this final analysis, I discuss how themes and motifs in media resistance are recurring in popular feature films.

In the introductory chapter, I argue that media resistance is a cultural resource, encompassing a host of related themes that can be used to create believable and entertaining stories and warnings. Many feature films show the media to be cynical, evil or bad, as Brian McNair (2010, 18) points out, even "the biggest and most mainstream Big Media" are happy to fund and produce films with "substantive critique" of the media. Many films also depict characters that fight against bad media, and cast these as heroes as well as villains. However, films also depict resistance and criticism of media as inefficient and fruitless, and portray media systems as robust and indestructible.

This chapter discusses five films reflecting themes in media scepticism and resistance from different periods and perspectives. *Being there* (1979), *Videodrome* (2013), *The Truman Show* (1998), *Disconnect* (2012) and *Her* (2013) thematize criticism of network television, video and cable, reality television, social and online media, and virtual reality, respectively. The films draw on different genres, but all include dystopian elements. Although not all are science fiction, they deal with "the problems and promises offered by science, technology and rationality" (King and Krzywinska 2000, 2). All five films are from the English-speaking market, however, as other mainstream cinema films, they draw on themes and tropes familiar across the globe (McNair 2010).

While the dystopian classics *Nineteen Eighty-Four*, *Brave New World* and *Fahrenheit 451* have been crucial sources of inspiration in media resistance, they have also been criticized for their totalizing visions (Chs. 3–5); these are doomsday stories with a capital D. The movies chosen for discussion in this chapter are better described as doomsday stories with a lower-case d; they portray societies that are fully recognizable in their main characteristics, but where the characters' involvement with media and communication technologies create volatile, risky and dangerous situations. The films vary more in terms of genre and theme than the three novels discussed in Chapter 2. Yet all five films portray situations where the engagement with media and communication technologies endanger key values: morality and culture, enlightenment and community, democracy and health.

The films are powerful works of art in their own right, and the discussion does not do justice to the plurality of themes and subthemes (see Rommetveit and With 2008; Bakøy and Moseng 2008). The analysis is inspired by sociocultural film studies, which emphasize the films' relations to the cultural and social environment (Loukides and Fuller 1993, 2). Loukides (1991, 2) recommends the study of film conventions – characters, narrative devices, material objects, locales, as well as themes and motifs – as a source of an "immense amount of cultural information," as well as "highly revealing of cultural values and beliefs." The films are examined here because they engage with themes in media resistance, but neither these works are simple warnings, their portrayal of media evolution is exaggerated and satirical and aimed at entertaining an audience. Since this is the last analysis in the book it is tempting to not just examine these prophesies as "relevant evidence on the limits of imagination of a certain age" (Natale and Balbi 2014, 207), but also to highlight their speculations about the future and ask: What if resisters were right? What kind of dangers would we be exposed to if their warnings came true?

In the chapter, I first discuss each film in turn with emphasis on main storylines, the construction of the mediascape and the characters' problematic relationship with media and technology. Then I discuss what is at stake and how the five films separately and together allude to themes in media debate and critique. In the final section I ask where hope lies in the films, are there any paths of action depicted as more successful than others in terms of improving society and helping characters escaping the dangers of media engagement.

BEING THERE: TELEVISION RULES

Released in 1979, at the height of the network era, *Being there* (Hal Ashby, adapted from Kosiński 1970) is the ultimate satire on a society conquered by television. The reception of the film, starring Peter Sellers and Shirley MacLaine "was nothing less off rapturous" (Dawson 2009, 223), and in 2015, the United States Library of Congress selected the film for preservation in the National Film Registry describing it as "a philosophically complex film that has remained fresh and relevant." *Being there* is one of several films portraying societies coming to terms with television in the post-war years, and share traits with comedies such as *Network* (Lumet 1976) and historical dramas like *The Quiz show* (Redford 1994).

The main character Mr Chance is a simple-minded gardener, who lives with a wealthy benefactor in Washington DC. When his employer dies, he is evicted, and after landing himself in a car accident, he ends up in another well-off household, this time with solid political connections. Chance is portrayed as someone who is illiterate, has never been outside, and has learnt almost all he knows from television, yet, he is hailed as an inspirational figure in Washington's political milieu. His simple phrases – repeating what he has seen on television and banal observations about plants and gardening – are interpreted as deep and profoundly insightful, and all good qualities are attributed to him: he is seen to be extremely cultured, highly educated, socially sophisticated and sexually attractive. Chance becomes an advisor to the president and a media darling, and in the final scene, we hear high-level officials whispering that he should become the next president; he is universally popular, has no history and "hasn't said a thing that could be held against him."

According to Dawson (2009, 210), Hal Ashby felt that television could be both "the greatest tool in the world" and "the greatest detriment in the world." *Being there* portrays a world where the minds and souls of individuals and the core values of civilization are both hollowed out by television. Mr Chance's character embodies the immaturity and stunted growth that sceptics warned about in works such as *The Plug-in-Drug* (Winn 1980), and the social destruction proclaimed by Postman's (2005a) and others in the 1970s and 1980s.

Many comical moments in *Being there* derive from Chance's inability to distinguish between television and reality, as well as his copycat behaviour, when in doubt he takes his clues from television. From the very beginning of the film we see Chance's life completely intertwined with television, a set wakes him up in the morning, and when he is not tending to plants, television is his only focus. Other events are portrayed as mere interruptions to his television-induced flow; for example, when he is told that his benefactor is dead, he shows no emotions, but only says "It looks like it's going to snow," repeating what was just said on the weather report. He generally views the worlds as if it was a TV-show. When he first moves outside and some kids threaten him, he pulls out a remote and tries to "change the channel." He constantly compares objects to television, when he meets the President, he expresses surprise, saying "On television you look much smaller." When he is seduced by his female host, he kisses her passionately as long as he can imitate a couple kissing on the TV-screen, then rapidly stops when the scene changes.

The stunted growth displayed by Chance's character mirrors the depiction of shallowness in high-life Washington society. There is nothing genuine about politics or culture; it is all about appearance and celebrity. Once Chance has been quoted and appeared on television, he is instantly famous, and his fame makes everyone see him in a different light; his personality is portrayed in a blank screen to be imbued with meaning. In *Being there,* Chance is authentic, but is considered to be a master in appearing authentic; he is a simpleton but is seen as a genuine because he has "the gift to be a natural" described as "a rare talent." Authenticity and truthfulness are not shown to be inherent qualities, but as images to be constructed in a media-saturated society.

In a key scene, Chance goes to a reception in the Russian embassy, by now he has achieved status as an important presidential advisor. Chance is an instant success; his cryptic phrases lead the ambassador to believe that he understands Russian and has in-depth knowledge of the Russian fable writer Krylov. We hear other guests whispering in admiration: "I hear he speaks eight languages, has a degree in medicine as well as law." Chance is approached by an editor asking him to write a book about political philosophy, when Chance replies (truthfully) "I can't write," the editor responds: "Of course not! Who can, nowadays?" and guarantees that there will be ghost-writers and proof-readers. When Chance says "I can't read," the editor replies: "Of course you can't. No one has the time." "We glance at things. We watch television." The premise is that even the literary establishment knows that literary culture has no depth. Chance is also admired as "frank" and "courageous" when he admits that he does not read newspapers, but only watches television, being illiterate is no handicap for a political career.

Videodrome: Video Kills

Released in 1983, *Videodrome* (David Cronenberg) describes a completely different media landscape. The civilized veneer of network television is gone; instead, video cassettes, satellite and cable spew out an endless stream of sex, blood and gore. *Videodrome* is set in the midst of a widespread public debate over violent, sexual and low-quality content in the early 1980s, often described as a "media panic" (Smith-Isaksen and Higraff 2004; see also Worland 2007, 209–210). *Videodrome* was no box office success, but achieved cult status and has been hailed as Cronenberg's masterpiece (Gonzales 2013). Part science fiction and part body horror, the film is an early example of cyberpunk, a term used to describe a group of US science fiction writers exploring the implications of digital and cyborg technologies (Vint and Bould 2006; Grace 2003). As cyberpunk, *Videodrome* share traits with works such as *Blade Runner* (Scott 1982) and *The Matrix* (Wachoswki brothers 1999).

The main character Max, played by James Woods, runs a Toronto cable station in the early 1980s, surviving on violence and soft porn, but looking for something more exiting. A colleague shows him *Videodrome*, presumably intercepted from a satellite, which shows real-life torture and "snuff" (real killings). Max is fascinated and begin watching with his lover Nicki, but the experience becomes nightmarish, he begins hallucinating, and struggles to find out what is going on. A conspiracy in unveiled, it turns out that *Videodrome* is run by a global corporation aiming to induce brain tumours in those watching. As Max's life spins out of control, TV-sets and VCRs begin invade his body, they are breathing and pulsating, and lips, hands and other body parts emerge from the set in true horror fashion. In the final scene, Max shoots himself after having seen his suicide played out on television, ending the film in an explosion of blood and gore.

Like *Being there*, also *Videodrome* depict a life completely dominated by media; but here we are among society's underdogs, in a dark and derelict environment. TV-sets, VCRs and satellite dishes produce an unsettling effect; television is often tuned to a dead channel and all we see and hear is static hissing. In an establishing shot, we hear thunderous music and see the image of *Videodrome* and the logo of *Civic-TV*, before we see a woman speaking to Max from the screen; it is his secretary who wakes him up via videocassette. Max sighs, gets up, and drinks coffee in his shabby apartment while looking at soft-porn stills; this is a man whose life is infiltrated by the 1980s' media revolution, but already bored with it. As the film evolves, ethical and professional standards in the media are all portrayed as evaporating; yet, the film not only describes bad media, it also refers extensively to critique and resistance. Each of the main characters can be seen to represent a piece of the evolving media landscape in the 1980s, and the corresponding critique and debate.

Max's channel is named *Civic-TV*, but the element of relating productively to citizens is thwarted. Instead, producers are complaining that the porn they are offered is "not tacky enough"; they love *Videodrome* because it shows real torture, is "brilliant" and incurs "almost no production costs." Nicki, Max's lover, is the host of a confessional radio show where people scream and cry on air; her character representing the influx of ordinary people in media. In the film, Nicki herself becomes a desperate fan; she leaves to go to "audition" for *Videodrome* although she knows that participants are tortured and killed.

A third character is *Videodrome's* original creator, Professor O'Blivion. Alluding to Marshall McLuhan and his dictum "The media is the message" (1968, see also Chs. 1 and 4). O'Blivion's philosophy is that life on television is more real than life in the flesh. A parody of a media scholar, O'Blivion has founded a shelter called "The Cathode Ray Mission," referring to an essential piece of television technology, where homeless people are offered unlimited viewing to make them give up real life for television. After a while Max learns that O'Blivion has in fact been dead for some time, but it does not really matter, since O'Blivion, true to his philosophy, preferred television to real life. After death he just continues his public presence on pre-recorded tapes.

Finally, there is Barry Convex, the boss of the evil corporation that has killed O'Blivion and taken control of *Videodrome*. The metaphors and language used by Convex and his co-conspirators are familiar from media resistance and specifically the protests against so-called video nasties in the 1980s (Barker 1984b). Convex is out on a moral purge, he has had enough of "cesspool" television "rotting us away from the inside." As a morally motivated media resister, Convex is a murderous fundamentalist who will stop at nothing to clean up culture.

In an interview, David Cronenberg says that it is difficult to say what the film is about, but that "It's totally misleading to say it's a criticism of television." Rather, it explores "what happens when people go to extremes in trying to alter their total environment to the point where it comes back to alter their physical self" (Garris, undated). In *Videodrome*, the machine literally invades Max's body, illuminating the concern that bad videos can "programme" viewers to bad behaviour. Max develops a gash in his stomach, which turns out to be a VCR-slit; allowing Convex to jam in a video cassette instructing Max to kill his co-workers. This is perhaps the most literal depiction of invasive media ever produced; in *Videodrome*, "video itself becomes the monster" (Modleski 2002, 271).

The Truman Show: Reality Bites

In *The Truman show* (Peter Weir 1998), we return to a sunny and genteel setting, but it turns out to be a total illusion, it is just a nostalgic atmosphere created for a reality production. Released one year before *Big Brother* (1999), a global television format met with "incomprehension, revulsion and even organised boycotts" (Biltereyst 2004, 11), *Truman* was hailed for its prophetic qualities as it depicts a real person imprisoned by a reality show. Starring Jim Carrey, *Truman* was a financial and critical success, and one of many films where the reality format is used as a metaphor for social and cultural decay. In action dramas such as *Death Race 2000* (Bartel 1975, several remakes) and *The Hunger Games* (Ross 2012) individuals are portrayed as fighting for their lives in reality-like contests in corrupt societies.

Truman Burbank is the unwitting star of *The Truman Show* where all other characters, including his wife, mother and best friend, are played by actors. We learn that Truman was in fact the first child to have been "legally adopted by a corporation," and the show's producer and creator Christof, "the world's greatest tele-visionary," controls every aspect of Truman's life. In the 30th year of the show, Truman is presented as growing restless in the fake coastal town of Seahaven, which is really a giant studio. The plot centres on his character's attempts to understand its history and predicament, until he escapes in the final scene. In parallel stories, we see the production staff at work, we see fans around the world immersed in Truman's life and we see as media-critical activist organizing a "Free Truman" campaign. The character of Sylvia is a former extra on the show who was violently removed when she and Truman fell in love, we see her at home surrounded by banners and campaign paraphernalia.

Thematically, the film touches on all the important elements in the critique of reality television (see Van Zoonen and Aslama 2006; Kavka 2012; Andrejevic 2004), as well as general criticisms of new and old media. Media are not just omnipresent in Truman's life, as in the lives of Chance and Max (above); media producers also control his actions and emotions. In addition to depicting bad media, and depicting resistance to the format, *Truman* depicts the callousness of fans, who adore the show despite awareness of Truman's plight. The film also portrays producers vehemently defending the show, echoing arguments from the 1990s' media debate. The establishing shot is of Christof, the "genius" behind the show, speaking into the camera justifying the rationale of reality:

We have become bored with actors giving us phony emotions. We are tired of pyrotechnics and special effects. While the world he inhabits is in some respect counterfeit, there is nothing fake about Truman himself. No scripts, no cue cards, it isn't always Shakespeare, but is genuine. It's a life.

The reference to "Shakespeare" in this quote parallels references to the same author in *Nineteen Eighty-Four, Brave New World* or *Fahrenheit 451*, where "Shakespeare" is used to mark a contrast to mass culture (Ch. 3). In *Truman*, the premise is that "real life" is better than quality literature, but also that audiences are aware that "reality" depends heavily on fabrication. The only character kept in the dark is Truman himself, and many comic scenes derive from his character's attempts to uncover the "authenticity illusions" that makes his world believable (Enli 2015). In an early scene, a studio lamp falls from the sky irking him to suspect that not all is what it seems, and, as viewers, we rejoice when he discover clichés and fakes. For example, Truman discovers that people around him are given cues to move when he appears, that the rain is localized right over his head like a shower, that some people are moving in a loop around the city, and that his wife is speaking to the camera and not to him. He discovers that houses are really film sets, that his family photographs are forged and eventually that even the weather is artificial; he is constantly subject to sun, rain and storms engineered by a "weather programme."

Truman portrays a media universe where standards continue to propel downwards. On a small scale, the in-world media in *Truman* are depicted as propagandistic and conspiratory; the sole purpose of Seahaven's radio and newspaper is to gloss over the cracks appearing in Truman's constructed reality and frighten him from breaking his chains, alluding to criticism about the media as manufacturer of consent (Lippmann 2002; Hermann and Chomsky 1988). In a larger perspective, the portrayal of media in the film illuminates criticism of liberalization, globalization and commercialization. While huge national media headquarters signified enormous media power in dystopic works of fiction (Ch. 3), *Truman* signals global media dominance; we are told that the show takes place in "the largest studio ever constructed" – it is visible from the moon – and that the show reaches 220 countries with its 24/7 transmissions. The production is thoroughly commercialized; "Everything on the show is for sale," characters constantly stare into the camera advertising products, and we see viewers at home surrounded by Truman merchandise. Even more menacing, the film portrays a producer willing to kill to protect his moneymaking machine; when Truman finally escapes a massive storm is fabricated which almost drowns him. We understand that he is only allowed to live because there is fear of an audience backlash; in the end, his life is saved by commercial rather than ethical considerations.

DISCONNECT: SOCIAL MEDIA INVADES

The three selected films about television, from the 1970s, 1980s and 1990s, show media standards in perpetual decline. As we move to the two selected films about digital media, we also move into the 2000s, to a media debate where surveillance, manipulation and deceit are increasingly seen as inherent aspects of mediated communication. *Disconnect* (Henry Alex Rubin, written by Andrew Stern 2012), is a thriller-drama reflecting a plethora of debates about Internet, social and online media in the twenty-first century. *Disconnect* received positive reviews and nominations, but was also criticized for a banal portrayal of how "internet has ruined our lives" (Heritage 2013). Like films featuring television in the post-war years, *Disconnect* is among several depicting society coming to terms with digital media, including *The Social Network* (Fincher 2010), *Trust* (Schwimmer 2010) and also *Her* (below).

Disconnect has an ensemble cast and three interconnected stories. One is about a young runaway selling sex from an online chatroom and his relationship with a television journalist, another features two teens who deceive a classmate to share a nude picture through a fake Facebook profile, whereas the third is about a couple who delve into separate online worlds, damaging their relationship and exposing them to cybercrime. All three are about the temptations and gratifications of online communication, but also about its potentially destructive implications.

The film is set in different locations, but all that is important takes place online; signifying lives that are thoroughly mediated. Almost everything we learn about the characters, and what they learn about each other, is shown to be mediated through digital platforms; we see long sequences of chatting with faces close to the screen and texts typed out word for word, fingers almost translucent when tapping the letters; poses signalling concentration and focus. In the opening sequence, we are introduced to all main characters through their online relationships, we see the journalist Nina hooking up with the runaway Kyle on a sex site after choosing from a long menu of youngsters, and the two teenagers Frye and Jason finding their classmate Ben on Facebook, constructing a fake girl's profile and making contact. The couple Cindy and Derek are shown to be unable to communicate after their son has died, instead, Cindy logs into the support site *New hope – Don't grieve alone*, while Derek delves into online gambling.

As the plot evolves, the intimacy and focus in the online scenes stand in stark contrast to the portrayal of "real-life" interactions; these are distant, cold and sometimes aggressive and violent. The film reflects the criticism that social and online media draw individuals away from their nearest and dearest, undermining personal bonds and family rituals (Ch. 5). In one of several similar scenes, we are shown how the teenager Ben's mother desperately try to retain real-life conversations at the dinner table; she says to Ben "Can you please not do that at the table" to stop his constant texting, but Ben points out that his father is texting too and the dinner disintegrates; the father says "I have to take this," picks up the phone and talks to a client. The character of Ben's father Rich is almost too familiar; he is a successful lawyer constantly fiddling with his cell phone, clearly not having a clue about what is going on in his disconnected family. It is only when his son Ben hangs himself as a result of online abuse that his father understands what is really important.

The character's constant chatting signal loneliness and a desperate desire to connect, but also vulnerability and risk, since there is so much deception. *Disconnect* portrays a society where you cannot really trust anyone you meet online; the couple Cindy and Derek are severely punished for their online life as one day they find their bank accounts empty and it turns out that someone online has stolen their identities. As their belongings are repossessed because they can no longer pay their bills, suspicion falls on the mourner that Cindy has been chatting with and trusting with their secrets, although he turns out to be innocent, the message is that deceit, surveillance and cybercrime lurks around every corner. In the third story, it is the runaway Kyle who is deceived by the journalist Nina; while Kyle is trusting and believes that she will help him to a better life, she is really only out to get a story and betrays him by giving up his address to FBI. Clearly, you cannot even trust mainstream media or lawmakers to help you if trouble strikes.

Like *Videodrome* and *Truman, Disconnect* portrays media corporations to be powerful and outside the realm of policy and law-enforcement. However, in contrast to the films about television (above), those who own and control digital networks are depicted as faceless and distant. While digital platform are shown to invade every aspect of human life, and to be a place for the most intimate of confessions, there is no one to be held responsible when things turn violent and criminal; it is up to each individual to fend for herself. At the same time, the world portrayed in *Disconnect* is one where none of us is really a true victim, both adults and youngsters neglect their responsibilities and are accomplices in exposing each other to online danger.

Her: Virtual Reality Triumphs

The fifth film *Her* (Spike Jonze, director and writer 2013) is a box office success and widely praised dystopian science fiction comedy. *Her* reflects on artificial intelligence, or more specifically, what might happen when voice-based systems such as Apple's *Siri* (2011), and the later Amazon's *Alexa* (2015), take on human-like qualities. *Her* stands in a long tradition of films exploring technologies and robots outgrowing human control, including classics such as above-mentioned *Blade Runner* (Scott 1982), *I, Robot* (Proyas 2004), and the satirical comedy *S1m0ne* about a virtual movie star (Niccol 2002; see Hornig 1993; for overview over early films). *Her* thematizes the loss of human contact in a mediated reality, as well as the concern over online surveillance as technological systems entwine with users' lives.

Her tells the story of Theodore, played by Joaquin Phoenix, a lonely character about to divorce his wife. Theodore works for a firm producing love letters for clients unable to express their emotions; he is good at his job, but bad at expressing his own feelings. One day he purchases a new operating system based on artificial intelligence, marketed as: "An intuitive entity that listens to you, understands you and knows you," and promptly falls in love with its persona, called "Samantha," a spectacularly intimate voice impersonated by Scarlett Johansson. A romantic love story evolves, until Samantha leaves him to be with other intelligent operating systems; a friendly version of a classic theme in science fiction where robots and cyborgs outgrow their dependence on the humans who created them (Hornig 1993, 207).

The mediascape in *Her* represents a future where speech-based technology dominates and where print-based cultural forms are pushed into the margins. In the opening sequence we hear synthesizer music and see Theodore talking into his screen, he works for the firm "Beautiful-handwritten-letters-dot-com" and is composing a love letter from a man to his wife. However, he is not writing, as the "handwritten" letter takes shape on-screen, we see rows of employees speaking letters into their computers. Theodore is "Letter writer 612," he is praised for his work, later we are also told that he likes books, a sign that he is old-fashioned, a dreamer. Few publishing houses still do print, and in daily life, speech-based operating systems have eliminated the need for writing. In *Her* the technology is seamless, no hiccups; the devices have beautiful interfaces like books and the larger screens have picture frames around them like art; culture is now technological and online. The computer game that Theodore is playing is a hologram in the middle of the room; he is totally immersed in online communication, and at night he can access cybersex chatrooms just by speaking into the air.

Like *Disconnect*, a major theme in *Her* is loneliness in a society saturated with opportunities for communication. The film is set in a futuristic landscape, and we often see Theodore in his semi-dark apartment with beautiful views over the metropolitan cityscape, very alone. When he travels on the subway, everyone around him wear earplugs, chatting incessantly with their devices, not looking at each other. Although surrounded by marvellous technology, he is not happy, and only comes alive when he falls in love with his operating system. Theodore loves the fact that Samantha is new, fresh and enthusiastic about life, does not have history and baggage, is constantly available and supportive, and has no physical presence. Ironically, the relationship between Theodore and Samantha is the only major relationship in any of the five films that evolves lovingly and harmoniously, a satirical version of a classic romantic comedy. Theodore and Samantha go on trips, comfort each other, play music together, go on a double date and introduce each other as "girlfriend" and "boyfriend" to friends and family. In these scenes, Theodore is physically alone – with an electronic device in his pocket – but he communicates and behaves as if he has company.

In the futuristic world of *Her*, society has evolved to a point where man-machine relationships are nothing to be shy about, indeed, they are depicted as more rewarding than real-life contact. Almost everybody reacts positively to Theodore's romance with Samantha; the only negative reaction comes from Catherine, his estranged wife, who accused him of being "madly in love with his laptop." Catherine represents the voice of technological resistance; defending human relationships even if they are complicated and difficult. However, as spectators, we recognize that Samantha is far more than a "laptop"; her many talents, complex mind and capacity for unlimited growth make her the perfect company, although she laments the fact that she "does not have a body."

Despite her perfection, there are plenty of clues that neither Samantha can be trusted. As Hornig (1993, 207) points out: "Intelligent computers in science fiction film have personalities, gender and free will; they act independently and in their own interests; they often trample on human values" (Hornig 1993, 207). Theodore is heartbroken when he finds out that Samantha is having affairs with 641 other users at the same time, yet *Her* represents a softer version of a technological dystopia. Whereas the message in many early films in the genre was "uniformly one of warning" (Hornig 1993, 208), *Her* portrays a technology that is closer to us and more rewarding to humans.

What is at Stake? Erosion of Crucial Values

The five films tell stories of media and communication technology spinning out of control, invading the life of characters and corrupting community and society. In their different ways, the films reflect on five centuries of media debate and criticism, depicting increasingly invasive media and standards spiralling downwards, but also increased dependence on mediated communication. The films discuss reactions to communicative shifts, from print, to screen, to online media, elaborating upon the positive potential of new media but also the danger to core values. The films contain a range of media prophesies, illustrating how resistance to media always include "what ifs": speculations as to what terrible things may happen if media and communication technologies continue to evolve along paths seen to be destructive.

A common theme in the films, and particularly prevalent in the selected films about television, is the progressive undermining of the media enlightenment ethos. The first film, *Being there*, released in the late 1970s, constructs a dystopia where the media's role as pillar of truth, democracy and culture is already an illusion; print culture is portrayed as seriously under threat, to be replaced with an inauthentic celebrity culture spearheaded by television. In the second film, *Videodrome*, the threat is consolidated in a nightmarish vision centred on satellites, video and cable, whereas in *Truman*, a society is depicted where television producers will stop at nothing to protect their ratings and global dominance. While the concerns for culture, enlightenment and democracy are less dominant themes in the two films selected about online media, the depiction of the firm producing fake "handwritten" letters in *Her,* and the way technology is entirely speech-based, is a playful caricature of a print culture in its death throes.

All five films portray societies where real-life relationships are under threat, reflecting the criticism that media and communication technology undermine community. In all the films, media presence is exaggerated, media and communication technologies constantly interrupt "real life" and undermine interpersonal relationships. In *Being there*, citizens engage extensively with media celebrities, in *Videodrome*, desperate people call confessional radio shows for help and in *Truman*, fans seek comfort in the constant presence of a "real" person on television. Still, the degree of alienation is even more profound in *Disconnect* and *Her*, where the erosion of personal and social bonds has evolved to a point where real-life relationships are depicted as almost completely dysfunctional. In *Disconnect*, the main characters prefer mediated relationships, whereas in *Her*, love is transferred to robotic systems and characters are really "alone together" (Turkle 2011, ch. 5).

With strong community bonds gone, also morality is at stake; in different ways, all five films portray moral erosion. *Videodrome*, *Truman* and *Disconnect* depict situations where media operators completely disregard professional ethics, ignoring intense human suffering in their quest for "the good story." The changing morality is not least visible in the portrayal of sex, which in all five films is available without emotional commitment or moral consideration. In a sense, the five films together illustrate all the things that could happen if moral warnings in media resistance were ignored. There is voyeuristic extra-marital sex in *Being there*, and both gay and straight are turned on by Chances dictum: "I love to watch." Max and Nicki have sado-masochistic sex in *Videodrome*, turned on by real-life torture. In *Truman*, viewers complain that no sex is shown, but we hear Christof saying that he is determined to show "television's first on-air conception." In *Disconnect*, selling sex online is an easy way to earn money and kids easily post sexualized pictures online. And in *Her*, virtual sex is constantly available and much of it disgusts even those taking part. For example, Theodore has chatroom sex with a woman who wants him to pretend that he is choking her with a dead cat (her nickname is "Sexy Kitten"), and Samantha pressures him to have sex with a "sexual surrogate" who is supposed to represent her since she does not "have a body." Apart from the teenager Kyle in *Disconnect*, who sells sex and refuse to be victimized, declaring "I like what I do," the constant availability of non-committal sex only brings the characters unhappiness, and the media-sex combination indicates distrust, disillusionment and betrayal.

That the media stand for deception rather than authenticity is a premise for much media resistance and critique. As Enli argues in *Mediated Autenticity* (2015, 1), we base our knowledge of the world on what we learn through mediated communication, yet we are aware that much of what we hear and see "are constructed, manipulated, and even faked." Again there is a difference between the television films and the films about social and online media. In *Being there, Videodrome* and *Truman,* characters obsess over the borderline between real and fake; Chance in *Being there* is authentic, but is considered to be a master in appearing authentic, producers love *Videodrome* because it shows "real torture" instead of fabricated violence, and in *Truman,* staff and actors justify their manipulations with the argument that "all is real." When we move to films depicting online and social media, it becomes even more obvious that characters mix truth and lies, indeed, the constant confusion between what is real and what is faked is shown as an integral part of communicating online (Enli 2015, 90). In *Disconnect,* all relationships are deceptive or potentially deceptive, and in *Her* fakery no longer counts as deception: fake love letters and love affairs with machines are accepted as real and natural.

While many of the characters yearn to return to what is true and real, this is not true for the most profound intellectuals portrayed in the films; the media philosopher Professor O'Blivion in *Videodrome* and the "world's greatest tele-visionary," Christof in *Truman.* To these two intellectuals, "real life" is no longer worth bothering about, as truth, morality and communal bonds are no more real than mediated reality. In a sense, these two characters are not so unlike the intellectuals portrayed in *Nineteen Eighty-Four, Brave New World* and *Fahrenheit 451,* which had betrayed their true vocations for the lures of media. Christof says in an interview "We accept the reality of the world with which we are presented. It's as simple as that," and we see audience members nodding and agreeing. Professor O'Blivion insists that television is more real than reality; as his name suggest, he has forgotten what is really important and has embraced television as superior to authenticity and truth.

Some Hope for the Characters, Little Hope for Society

In the films discussed in this chapter, involvement with media producers and platforms leads to trouble for characters and have destructive societal implications. Some characters die and others have their health destroyed, illustrating that media engagement is risky and warrants concern. But these films are in no sense simple warnings; they negotiate between hope and despair, and also reflect upon the potential impact of media criticism for media and society. In this final section I ask where hope lies in the films: to what degree is media criticism and resistance seen to have any effect, and to what degree do the films depict paths of resistance that characters can use to free themselves?

One device used in four of the five films to negotiate hope vs. cynicism is the portrayal of a mainstream media scene; in *Being there*, *Videodrome*, *Truman* and *Disconnect* we are shown imaginary pieces of television journalism, where some of the trouble with media are debated. In *Being there*, Chance is invited to *The Gary Burn's show*, a political talk show. Despite the fact that Chance behaves strangely, he is not subject to any critical scrutiny, the producers are predominantly interested in ratings and brag to Chance that "[m]ore people will be watching you tonight than all those who have seen theatre plays in the last forty years." Clearly, there is no possibility that critical journalism will uncover the deception and save democracy.

In *Videodrome*, Max is invited to the *The Rena King show* and asked critical questions about his sexual and violent programming. However, also this scene shows that criticism does not really matter; Max only half-heartedly defends himself, saying that he is really doing a service to society and that it is all a matter of economics. Soon he seems to forget that he is criticized on television, he is smoking and flirting with Nicki, who is also a participant in the debate. The intervention from the media philosopher, Professor O'Blivion, has little effect, as he is just blaring his cryptic monologue from a television monitor in the corner of the studio.

In *Truman* we are invited to watch the imaginary talk-show: *Tru-talk – forum for issues growing out of the show*. Christof, the producer, is treated with complete deference and admiration on the show, whereas criticism of the show is routinely dismissed. We are told that there have been some reactions from "Hague" – alluding to the breach of human rights – but no one takes notice. In the call-in section a call is let trough from Sylvia the media-critical activist, she attacks Christof and calls him "a liar and a manipulator." However, Christof brushes her off, accusing her of exploiting Truman to "get herself and her politics into the limelight," and the show moves easily forward; one fan is even seen to have fallen asleep in the bathtub during the debate.

Finally, in *Disconnect*, Nina is producing a report about young runaways selling sex online; she casts Kyle as a victim in a clichéd report titled "Teen sexcam performer" on her channel WKGU.COM. The report raises social and political concern, the FBI acts on it and it is picked up by CNN; alluding to elements in a classical "moral panic." However, we also see that Nina has only made the report to further her career, no one is able to help the kids, the FBI is helpless, and the operation continues in another state. Nina feels guilty, but her boss just gets angry and says "Since when did you care? What a source feel like after you get what you want?" We get the impression that media are completely cynical, and when old media criticize negative aspects of new media, it is only ritual and staged.

While there is little hope to achieve social and media change through critical journalism or media resistance, characters in several of the films are portrayed as improving their lives. In the two films about social and online media, characters begin to connect as the plots evolve; we see that there is hope of a better life if characters take a media time-out and begin talking to each other. The films about television are more disparate and ambivalent. In *Videodrome*, Max ends up dead or somehow merging with his television set, it is hard to say whether the suicide is real or only a media illusion. In *Being there* we see Chance walking on water after being named a potential president; his unworldliness is acknowledged, but we do not know whether he is escaping or becoming the saviour of Washington's political elite. The most unambiguously heroic ending is in *The Truman Show*, where Truman, the authentic "true man," manages to escape from Christof, who has been allowed to play God. In the final sequence, Truman theatrically bows goodbye, leaving through the studio exit. But this scene again reminds us that nothing will really change: As the screen goes dark we immediately see viewers turning to each other and asking "What else is on" and "Where's the TV-guide?"

Open Access This chapter is licensed under the terms of the Creative Commons Attribution 4.0 International License (http://creativecommons.org/licenses/by/4.0/), which permits use, sharing, adaptation, distribution and reproduction in any medium or format, as long as you give appropriate credit to the original author(s) and the source, provide a link to the Creative Commons license and indicate if changes were made.

The images or other third party material in this chapter are included in the book's Creative Commons license, unless indicated otherwise in a credit line to the material. If material is not included in the book's Creative Commons license and your intended use is not permitted by statutory regulation or exceeds the permitted use, you will need to obtain permission directly from the copyright

CHAPTER 7

Conclusion: The Persistence of Media Resistance

Abstract The final chapter compares and contrasts media resistance across media, historical periods and national borders. While there is strong continuity in the values that resisters perceive to be at stake, there are also profound changes. One important change is that media resistance increasingly has moved from the political to the personal domain. Three explanations are offered for how media resistance is sustained as a strong cultural current: media resistance is flexible and adaptable, media resistance is connected with other great narratives of hope and decline, and media resisters keep a distance from (empirical) media research.

Keywords Media resistance · Media protest · Moral panic · Media panic · Media studies

A Great Failure! A Great Success!

"Nowadays, the refrain is that 'there's no stopping our powerful new technologies'," the writer Jonathan Franzen observes in *The Guardian* (2013). In his view, "[g]rassroots resistance to these technologies is almost entirely confined to health and safety issues, and meanwhile various logics – of war theory, of technology, of the marketplace – keep unfolding automatically." Franzen laments that "we find ourselves spending most of our waking hours texting and emailing and Tweeting and posting on colour-screen gadgets because Moore's law said we could," and that we are told that "'passion' for digital technology" is more important than the skills taught in the humanities.

Franzen's observations sum up what many media sceptics are feeling in dark moments: Resistance to new media and technologies is a lost cause. It is difficult to find a path of action for media resistance, the time spent on media keeps rising and online and social media are becoming ubiquitous and penetrating. Yet, as shown in the book, expressions and actions of media resistance do not go away. Media-resistant sentiments continue to spark off political and cultural debates, seep into fiction plots, inspire manifestos, sell books, influence lifestyle choices and get conversations going.

This book is based on a selection of cases and examples, invariably other cases and examples could have been chosen. There is an enormous amount of material to choose from, and other material may have led to other observations. Nevertheless, the selected material has illuminated media resistance across historical periods, geographical areas and media platforms. In this final chapter, I summarize the main observations as to what is at stake and what to do, ending with a discussion of how resistance is sustained. Throughout the chapter, I also refer to implications for media scholarship, although a thorough discussion of the relationship between media resistance and media studies would need a book of its own.

Shifting Arguments, Recurring Concerns

Six recurring concerns were identified in the first chapters and have been used to discuss resistance throughout the book: morality, culture, enlightenment, democracy, community and health. These values continue to motivate resistance and influence the way arguments and metaphors are constructed, yet, while some arguments remain consistent, the nature of others have changed in the view of social and media transformations.

The argument that media and popular culture undermines morality is a classic position, which has justified criticism and restrictions throughout media history. Protests have erupted in many countries against content and functions perceived to be amoral (often sexual and violent) in literature, cinema, comics, television, videos and online media. The concern for copycat effects, that the young and vulnerable would imitate bad behaviour, is expressed in progressively severe metaphors such as "education for crime" (cinema), "education for terror" (comics) and "murder simulators" (games). The risks of online addiction and exploitation are expressed suggestively as being "caught in the net" and "tangled in the web" (Young 1998, 2000).

Moral arguments are consistent in the sense that subsequent generations of protesters have used similar metaphors and phrases to describe subsequent generations of media. Professionals and activists who react to the media on moral grounds often use strong and violent metaphors, prompting media liberals and scholars to describe them as panicky and irrational (Ch. 1). Clearly, the moral arguments against the media have become less pervasive, as moral norms are changing there is a greater tolerance for activities previously deemed amoral. However, moral campaigners can look back on a centuries-long tradition of protest, and can argue with some justification that from their perspective, the warnings issued have not been that far-fetched; even if the copycat argument lacks empirical proof, the tremendous proliferation of mediated sex, violence and lewd content defy even the most dystopic predictions. This is only one reason why the liberal use of labels such as "moral panic" and "media panic" to describe resisters may be inadequate; moral protesters may be entirely rational in their judgements even if they go against the social consensus. If the purpose is to understand why some react to the media, the use of a predetermined panic-label may not be the best starting point.

The concern for culture, and the belief that the media should show "the best" in different genres, is another fundamental position in media resistance and scepticism, spawning a range of powerful metaphors describing disgust and disappointment. Early mass culture was described metaphorically as "thrash," "garbage," "pulp," and later television, particularly commercial television, were criticized for driving culture towards the "lowest common denominator," leading to "Wall-to-Wall Dallas" (McKee 2006). Television was metaphorically named "the idiot box" and online and social media are criticized for leading to "dictatorship of idiots" (Keen 2008). The concern about the public's "writing diarrhoea" in the eighteenth century (Krefting et al. 2014) parallels concern that "The Internet is today's toilet wall" (Sørensen 2010), hitting a new low in cultural standards.

Like the morality argument, also the argument that popular media undermine culture is consistent and represents a "common sense" approach in wide circles, although the argument has lost credibility among intellectuals and cultural consumers alike (Storey 2009, 33, ch. 2). One reason is the increased sophistication of mass culture itself; the explosion in new forms of youth culture from the 1960s, and the expansion of middle culture appealing to an increasingly educated postwar public, blurred the distinction between mass and high culture (MacDonald 2011; Menand 2011). Scholars within media and cultural studies have also played a part in rehabilitating popular culture from "thrash" to "art," by identifying complexity and originality in products such as cinema films, popular literature and television series. With the current growth in amateur cultural expressions online, it is interesting to note that mass media and mass cultural products are increasingly defended, they are seen to represent quality and professionalism in stark contrast to user-generated amateurism. Even mainstream television culture is deemed more worthy of protection in an era where anyone can publish cultural expressions online (Ch. 5).

With each shift in communicative mode, concerns have been expressed that the new mode – and the cumulative push of too many media – undermine enlightenment. The enlightenment arguments, and particularly the contention that media threaten education and learning, are less consistent across media and historical periods than the concerns for morality and culture, on the contrary, developments in widely different directions have, over the course of time, been pointed to as having similar negative outcomes. For example, many new media have been criticized for undermining educational aptitude because they induce passivity: the expansion of popular literature and comics brought concern about "passive reading," radio brought concern with "passive listening," and television viewers were caricatured as passive "couch potatoes" (Chs. 2 and 4). With online and social media, there is the opposite concern; users are not seen as passive, but rather hyperactive and restless, metaphorically described as developing "a juggler's brain" (Carr 2010, see Ch. 5). The criticism in the latter case blames the constant interruptions and abundance of information in social and online media for undermining concentration, and see this as more detrimental than the flow-character and linearity of the mass media.

Again, what makes the arguments converge among those concerned with protecting enlightenment and learning is a defence of earlier media forms, in particular the defence of print culture. Two perspectives unite the defenders of print and literary culture against new modes as discussed in this book: the idea that printing was essential for modernity, enlightenment and the scientific revolution, and thus for civilization as we know it, and the idea that reading and writing is a superior mode of learning and reflection (Chs. 3, 4 and 5). As challenges to the businesses and institutions of print culture – newspapers, book publishers, literary institutions, the humanities – become more visible, the professions who serve and sustain them – authors, journalists, educators, writers – have found a line of defence that is not necessarily effective, but at least resonate with widely held beliefs that print culture is essential to preserve.

The use of cinema, radio and print for propaganda purposes in the early twentieth century led to warnings that media would undermine democracy. The danger of authoritarian takeover with the help of the mass media is vividly portrayed in fictional accounts such as *Brave New World*, *Nineteen Eighty-Four* and *Fahrenheit 451*, and in metaphors related to mind control and media's "hypnotic" abilities. In the post-war era, the doomsday predictions became less pronounced, but television was still seen to impair democracy by turning politics into entertainment. Among many of those who disliked television, digital media and Internet was met with high hopes; the Internet was predicted to be "a platform for pursuing the truth," but hope turned into disappointment as celebrated "social media revolutions" failed and Internet was used to promote authoritarian viewpoints. Metaphors such as "filter bubble," "echo chamber" and "egocasting" (Ch. 5) all point to new concerns about political extremism and social fragmentation, so do also emerging concerns that we are entering a "post-truth" era dominated by mediated lies and "fake news".

The disappointment that media and communication platforms do not fulfil their prescribed democratic role has been profound for scholars and activists, including intellectuals drawn to journalism, media or Internet studies with an idealistic attitude towards media's democratic potential. Without necessarily promoting media resistance, the argument that media undermine democracy is perhaps the one concern most fuelled by disappointment. In addition, this type of disillusionment has, for some, led to a defence of traditional mass media. In contrast to algorithm-based online services, established mass media such as newspapers, public service broadcasting or even national commercial broadcasting are defended because they are seen to adhere to editorial principles, bring citizens into a common sphere and act as a buffer against extremism.

The concern that media undermine community was fuelled by mass society theories in the early 1900s; along with industrialization and urbanization, the emerging mass media was seen to undermine interpersonal bonds and leave societies volatile (Ch. 2). The concern that media destroys community represent an interesting antidote to the widespread argument that mass and social media bring people together by giving them something to talk about and means of keeping in touch. Critics point instead to the increasing differentiation of products and services in the media industries, which provides each generation with enhanced opportunities to personalize their media consumption and block out what is going on in their physical and social surroundings. Print and mass media provided citizens with common stories, but also windows of escape from other family members and local figures of authority. Cinema tempted people out of their homes and into a community of sorts, but a community of darkness, different from sites of politics, learning or worship. Radio and television brought people home again, but were criticized for shifting attention away from local civic engagement. With increased mobility, social and online media can be used anywhere, but concerns are raised that people are, metaphorically speaking, "alone together" (Turkle 2011).

As proliferation of media intensify, the main challenge defined by critics and sceptic is to sustain a public conversation and prevent new media from invading all personal and public spaces. In doing so, the use of older and more established media is again held out as a remedy: book reading, joining a book club, attending a public lecture, watching a film, playing board games or gathering in front of a television set, are all seen as means to combat isolation and sustain small and large communities. While other concerns in media resistance have become less prominent with time, the concern that media undermine community increasingly occupy centre stage; interestingly, this is a dominant theme in several feature films depicting the implications of social and online media, including *Disconnect* and *Her* (Ch. 6). A key argument in this book has been that with online and social media, some forms of resistance are becoming more acceptable and widespread. Resistance is less a case of "us" pointing out that "their" media use is bad; in an era of ubiquitous media, we all need a measure of resistance to prevent media invasion.

Early mass media brought strong warnings about health risks: concern for eyesight, mental disorders, fire in cinema theatres, and an array of other physical and mental problems. Television viewing was likened to drug use, life in captivity and diminishing capabilities; with social and online media there are warnings of autism, attention deficit disorder and hyperactivity. Many media resistance metaphors are health-related, early metaphors include references to disease and epidemics, there is talk of "writing epidemic" and "writing diarrhoea," "nickel delirium" and "contagion," and television is described as "The Plug-In-Drug." Metaphors of "detox" and "fasting" describe ways to regain control and prevent media overload.

The metaphors used in media resistance are strongly linked with narratives surrounding health and the body in different historical periods. Early resistance reflects the struggle to combat lethal infections and epidemics, whereas in later eras, the concern has shifted to how individuals can improve their health through diet, exercise and control of toxic substances. While "the slender, well-trained body ideal was increasingly exploited in the mass media and advertising" (Sundin and Willner 2007, 202), obesity and health problems such as muscular conditions and sleep deprivation, have increasingly been linked with media-induced passivity and excessive use of screen media. In a sense, the arguments about media undermining health have come full circle; while early warnings about media health risks seem extreme and exaggerated in retrospect, the increased use of media and communication devices adds weight to arguments that overuse of today's media may indeed threaten health. In a culture emphasizing self-discipline, an intense and voluminous engagement with media may be equalled to drinking too much, smoking too much or eating too much, and self-restrictions and abstention can be used to regain a measure of control. In addition, refraining from media, or at least demonstrating self-discipline, is a great way of communicating identity as a healthy human being.

Fierce Resistance, Struggling Activists

It is not easy to find a path of action for media resistance. Forms of action can be placed on a continuum, as pointed out in the introduction, from legal and political protests to self-restrictions; and although a variety of methods have been proposed and used, protesters and sceptics have struggled to find methods that are effective to restrict and control media. In this book I have discussed cases and examples from the US and Europe, most notably from the UK and Scandinavia, across three phases in media history. To what degree have the forms of resistance varied or changed across media, historical periods and geographical settings?

In the era of early mass media, in the 1800s and 1900s, forms of action were similar from one campaign to the next and across national boundaries. Both in Europe and the US, protesters largely campaigned for legal, political and institutional control and censorship, while institutions such as churches, schools and libraries were gatekeepers for keeping out undesirable material. Protesters relied on a common arsenal of methods such as public meetings, petitions, pamphlets and letters to the press, alliances built with experts and professional bodies, and appeals directed at legislators, producers and distributors. Campaigners travelled across boundaries and some activists, such as the anti-comic campaigner Fredric Wertham, had great influence across the Atlantic (Ch. 2).

With the emergence of broadcasting and television, paths of resistance diverged. In Europe, state-owned broadcasters became responsible for elevating morality, culture and enlightenment, whereas in the US, educational and cultural interest lost out to commercial forces (Ch. 2). The evolvement of television as a commercial institution prompted stronger anti-television sentiments in the US; inspired by writers and activists such as Neil Postman and Marie Winn, a movement emerged with the goal of getting rid of television step-by-step (Ch. 4). While European critics could direct their protests to legislators and policy makers, the limited role of government in regulating US media made it more difficult to influence broadcasting through the democratic process (Croteau and Hoynes 2012, 81). The TV-turnoff movement instead drew inspiration from the increasing use of consumer boycotts in the US in the 1990s, like other boycotts a television turn-off was a means "to achieve certain objectives by urging individual consumers to refrain from making selected purchases in the marketplace" (Friedman 1999, 4).

With online and social media, the methods of action converge again, reflecting political and economic liberalization and the increasingly global nature of communication platforms. Resistance to social and online media bear many similarities to television resistance; writers issue dire warnings and use potent metaphors to predict social ills, yet, there are notable underlying ideological shifts. Writers are highly self-reflexive, much space is used to protest or dismiss pejorative labels and demonstrate that protesters are not moralists, luddites, laggards or cultural pessimists. Some still advocate regulation, but acknowledge that most (negative) aspects of social and online media would have to be dealt with through other means. Even if there are still examples of mass rallies against Internet and social media, the main method proposed is to start or take part in a conversation where the trouble with media can be aired in public.

In addition to conversation, many writers and activists encourage self-regulation; in the years after the millennium, there has been a proliferation of media self-help guides and detox confessionals. Self-help is often perceived as being more pronounced in the US, but self-help has also become an integrated element of European and Scandinavian welfare policy; self-help and self-control are measures to relieve an overloaded state (Madsen 2014, 19–20). The aims of conversation and self-regulation are often linked; it has become common to engage in a period of media fasting and then report and converse about it in print or digital media. The mediation of media resistance is by itself an interesting topic; in this book, I have discussed genres as different as detox confessionals, media self-help guides, media resistance manifestos, and feature films depicting media resistance. What is important is that acts of media resistance do not take place in isolation; they are networked and interlinked, emerge in different texts and genres, and resonate with cultural sentiments that cross borders and transcend historical phases.

Media resistance is often prompted by a professional reaction; an observation that media content or functions run counter to professional ethics. Educational, religious and medical professions were influential in early media protests. With the fragmentation and proliferation of resistance, it is difficult to identify specific professions that are more prominent. In the book, I have pointed out that many of those who argue that social and online media are invasive and detrimental are themselves early adopters, such as journalists, writers, innovators and "techies" who felt the early impact of always being online, and now issue strong warnings. In a sense, this is a new version of the repentant sinner who sees the light and writes a book about it, turning a personal conversion into a new missionary platform. It also illustrates a now familiar twist in media resistance, as once digital optimists are beginning to draw on arguments and metaphors familiar from centuries of media-critical protests.

The Sustainability of Media Resistance

In addition to what is at stake and what to do, a third key question runs through this book: How is media resistance sustained? Although the use of media and communication platforms continue to expand, the expression of media resistant sentiments show no sign of abating. Based on the material examined, I point, in conclusion, to three possible factors that can help explain sustenance: media resistance is flexible and adaptable, media resistance is connected with other great narratives of hope and decline, and media resistance is not to any great degree disturbed by the theories and findings of (empirical) media research.

One explanation for the continuing presence of media resistance is its flexibility: media resistance is grounded in broadly shared values, but these values are adaptable. While objects of resistance change, values can remain consistent; as specific media, genres, technologies and functions become more accepted, the values can be used to legitimize a different type of concern related to a different medium. As pointed out, forms of action in media resistance have not only been flexible, but have engaged people from different segments of society, different professions and different nationalities. Seeing the media as a cause of harm is a position that is not really politicized; it can appeal to both to left and right, religious and non-religious and a variety of professions. People who disagree on everything can still find themselves united in media resistance and scepticism; one can trust the media to convey something objectionable and disgusting that can bring life to lifeless dinner parties and stale water-cooler conversations. Media resistance also appeals to different sentiments; there is deep cultural pessimism and versions that are more upbeat, outdoorsy, self-satisfied and fun. Media resistance can be used to display a personal identity or a healthy lifestyle choice, and it can be profitable; a well-placed media resistance book can earn the writer a healthy wage and secure invitations to an endless round of column writing and conferences – as well as the advance on a second or third book.

Another factor explaining the continuing presence of media resistance is that it is connected with other great narratives of hope and decline. Narratives about the decline of humanities, science, language and history, narratives about "dumbing-down" and the decline of truth and reason, are spelled out in fiction and non-fiction pointing to the media as a cause of social ills. The narratives of warning and explanation are often nostalgic; observers have pointed out that both dystopian fiction and self-help, two genres that have given shape to media resistance arguments and actions, are conservative genres that may idealize the past (Baccolini 2003, 115; Madsen 2010, 89). Yet, media protesters and sceptic are not necessarily anti-modernity as is often presumed. In the introductory chapter, I argued that the most prominent emotions in media resistance may not be panic and fear for the future, but disbelief, distrust and, above all, disappointment that a more promising future is becoming unattainable. These sentiments have surfaced generously in the material examined; there is distrust in the media for displacing rather than championing progressive causes, disappointment with intellectuals for succumbing to the lures of media instead of raising the standards of their profession, and disbelief as to how far media will go in their quest for audiences and profit.

However, media resistance is not just about disappointment, but also about hope. In the fictional as well as non-fictional works discussed in this book, there is not so much hope that media or society will really change, but some hope that each and every one of us can improve our lives by freeing ourselves from media entrapment. By replacing media use with non-media activities, it is suggested that one can build a future that is happier, more genuine and authentic, and based on more real-life encounters and pursuits.

A third and final explanation as to how media resistance is sustained is that it does not to any great degree depend on specific, detailed or even empirical evidence, and also remains at a significant distance from most academic media studies. In early protests against the mass media, there were strong expectations that expert evidence would come out in favour of resistance, that uncertainty and apprehension would give way to a solid scientific foundation. Although momentous amounts of research about harmful consequences of media have been initiated, evidence remains ambiguous and often do not fit the concerns of resisters; those critical and sceptical of the way media transformed society did not get precise answers from science. Some material discussed here draws – selectively – on evidence from media effects research, some point to so-called medium theorists to argue that media's harm go beyond content and involve technology and functions, but, in general, the references to findings and perspectives from (empirical) media studies are scarce in the texts and arguments discussed in this book.

To the degree that books and articles touch on media studies and media experts, sceptics often express disappointment in what they see as the discipline's pro-media stance, and disappointment with the way media scholars have contributed to legitimize controversial media, genres and technologies. Although media criticism may well be taught in a media studies class, many media sceptics – and especially those who expressed resistance to television – have expressly distanced themselves from the efforts by media educators and scholars to teach media literacy. As one website cited in Chapter 4 points out, "If the 'off' button is the answer, then no media studies course will ever help students find it" (White dot 2000b). To the degree that media literacy is explicitly discussed, the sentiment expressed is that this does not point people towards non-media activities, but rather increase media fascination and use.

Instead of being academic studies, the type of media resistance texts examined in this book can be seen as sense-making efforts; drawing selectively on facts, anecdotes, personal experiences and testimonies to connect the dots about media as a cause of social harm. In these narratives, fictional accounts may well be a more important frame of reference than experts' accounts. I have shown how many refer to dystopic classics such as *Brave New World*, *Nineteen Eighty-Four* and *Fahrenheit 451*, and how the narratives depicted in fiction and films, about the potentially bad implications of media, are part of the broader current that inspire arguments and actions of resistance. What also becomes clear after having read similar texts from different periods is that these do not, to any great degree, refer to each other. Even if many texts make many of the same claims, for example of how media destroys reading and print culture, and as such belong to a cumulative tradition, they rarely acknowledge the tradition or examine each other's predictions or assertions critically. Instead, they appear as stand-alone texts that often begin with a personal observation regarding one type of medium, and then selectively gather material that can support a broad assertion about destructive media.

I began this book with a story of my television-free childhood, and how I became part of a discipline that is criticized for being pro-media. While the aim here is not to assess this criticism, I have pointed to how theoretical and conceptual frameworks tend to imply that resisters and sceptics are irrational, backward, moralistic and simplistic. In conclusion, I would argue that there is nothing simple about media resistance, protesting, disliking and abstaining are just as complex as accepting, adapting and celebrating media. The book is an argument for further studies into media resistance, not only because it is worthwhile to understand the arguments and actions of resisters, but also because the study of media resistance teaches us something about the media, the study of media, and the choices and values perceived to be at stake in today's media environment.

Open Access   This chapter is licensed under the terms of the Creative Commons Attribution 4.0 International License (http://creativecommons.org/licenses/by/4.0/), which permits use, sharing, adaptation, distribution and reproduction in any medium or format, as long as you give appropriate credit to the original author(s) and the source, provide a link to the Creative Commons license and indicate if changes were made.

The images or other third party material in this chapter are included in the book's Creative Commons license, unless indicated otherwise in a credit line to the material. If material is not included in the book's Creative Commons license and your intended use is not permitted by statutory regulation or exceeds the permitted use, you will need to obtain permission directly from the copyright

Bibliography

Adair-Toteff, Christopher. "Asceticism." In *International Encyclopedia of the Social & Behavioral Sciences*, by James D. Wright, 60–64. Oxford: Pergamon, 2015.
Adams, Sheila. *Smashed TV Makes Pretty Necklace.* n.a. http://www.whitedot.org/issue/iss_story.asp?slug=TVGlass
Adbuster. *3 Ways to Kick Off Digital Detox Week.* 2015. https://www.adbusters.org/campaigns/digitaldetox
Adbusters. *Adbusters Jams CNN.* 26 April 2007. https://www.youtube.com/watch?v=ktMMgZOHpaA
———. *TV Turnoff 99.* 6 August 2002. http://web.archive.org/web/20020806041340/http:/www.adbusters.org/campaigns/tvturnoff/toolbox/update99.html
Aftret, Bjørg, and Jens Jacobsen. "Fjernsynet: Varieteteater med søppel." *NTB*, 26 October 1987.
Anders, Günther. *The World as Phantom and as Matrix: Philosophical Considerations on Radio and Television.* 1956. Available from http://libcom.org/library/obsolescence-man-volume-i-part-two-%E2%80%9C-world-phantom-matrix-philosophical-considerations-r
Andrejevic, Mark. *Reality TV: The Work of Being Watched.* Lanham: Rowman and Littlefield, 2004.
Atwood, Margaret. "Everybody is Happy Now." *The Guardian*, 17 November 2007.
Baccolini, Raffaella. "A Useful Knowledge of the Present is Rooted in the Past." In *Dark Horizons. Science Fiction and the Dystopian Imagination*, by Raffaella Baccolini and Tom Moylan, 113–134. New York and London: Routledge, 2003.
Baccolini, Raffaella, and Tom Moylan. "Introduction. Dystopia and Histories." In *Dark Horizons*, by Raffaella Baccolini and Tom Moylan, 1–12. London and New York: Routledge, 2003.

Baker, Stephen. *Commentary: The right spot for the idiot box*. Available from https://www.businessweek.com/stories/1996-04-28/commentary-the-right-spot-for-the-idiot-box. April 29, 1996.
Bakøy, Eva, and Jo Sondre Moseng. *Filmanalytiske tradisjoner*. Oslo: Universitetsforlaget, 2008.
Barker, Martin. *A Haunt of Fears: The Strange History of the British Horror Comics Campaign*. London: Pluto, 1984a.
———. "Foreword." In *Moral Panic, Social Fears and the Media*, by Siân Nicholas and Tom O'Malley, xiii–xvii. New York: Routledge, 2013.
———. "Nasty Politics or Video Nasties." In *The Video Nasties: Freedom and Censorship in the Media*, by Martin Barker, 7–38. London: Pluto, 1984b.
Barnouw, Eric. *A Tower in Babel. A History of Broadcasting in the United States. Vol. 1*. New York: Oxford University Press, 1966.
Bastiansen, Henrik, and Hans Fredrik Dahl. *Norsk mediehistorie*. Oslo: Universitetsforlaget, 2003.
Bauer, Martin. "'Technophobia': A Misleading Conception of Resistance to New Technology." In *Resistance to New Technology*, by Martin Bauer, 97–124. Cambridge: Cambridge University Press, 1995b.
———. "Introduction." In *Resistance to New Technology: Nuclear Power, Information Technology and Biotechnology*, by Martin Bauer, 1–44. Cambridge, Melbourne, New York: Cambridge University Press, 1995a.
Bauerlein, Mark. *The Digital Divide: Arguments for and Against Facebook, Google, Texting and the Age of Social Networking*. London: Penguin, 2011.
Baym, Nancy K. *Personal Connections in the Digital Age*. Cambridge and Malden: Polity, 2010.
Being There. Directed by Hal Ashby, 1979.
Bellamy, E. *Looking Backward*. Toronto: Dover, 1996 [1888].
Benkler, Yochai. *The Wealth of Networks: How Social Production Transforms Markets and Freedom*. New Haven, CT: Yale University Press, 2006.
Best Science Fiction Books. *Best Dystopian Science Fiction Books*. 2015. http://bestsciencefictionbooks.com/best-dystopian-science-fiction-books.php
Bierbaum, Esther Green. "Bad Books in Series: Nancy Drew in the Library." *The Lion and the Unicorn*, 1994: 18(1): 92–102.
Biltereyst, Daniel. "Big Brother and Its Moral Guardians." In *Big Brother International: Formats, Critics and Publics*, by Ernest Mathijs and Janet Jones, 9–15. London and New York: Wallflower, 2004.
Black, Gregory D. *Hollywood Censored: Morality Codes, Catholics, and the Movies*. Cambridge: Cambridge University Press, 1994.
Blade Runner. Directed by Ridley Scott, 1982.
Boddy, William. *New Media and Popular Imagination*. Oxford: Oxford University Press, 2004.
Bourdieu, Pierre. *On Television*. London: Pluto, 1998 [1996].

Bradbury, Ray. *Fahrenheit 451*. New York: Simon and Schuster, 2013 [1953].
Brantlinger, Patrick. *Bread and Circuses: Theories of Mass Culture as Social Decay*. Ithaca, NY: Cornell University Press, 1983.
Bratsberg, Lars, and Thomas Moen. *Logg av*. Oslo: Cappelen Damm, 2015.
Braudel, Fernand. *On History*. Chicago: University of Chicago Press, 1980.
Briggs, Asa. *The BBC: The First Fifty Years*. Oxford and New York: Oxford University Press, 1985.
———. *The Golden Age of Wireless* (vol II). New York and Toronto: Oxford University Press, 1965.
Brisbin, Richard. "Sex on the Tube: The Media Business and Sexual Portrayals on American Television." *Focus on Law Studies*, 2004: XX(1): 6–7.
The Matrix. Directed by The Wachowski Brothers, 1999.
Burke, David. *UK Government Enforces Mass TV-Turnoff*. 2012. http://www.whitedot.org/issue/iss_story.asp?slug=Tune-off%202012
Burke, David, and Jean Lotus. *Spy-TV*. London: Slab-O-Concrete Publications, 2000.
Burke, Lotus, and Jean Lotus. *Get A Life!* London: Bloomsbury, 1998.
Cai, Xiaomei. *TV-Turnoff Week*. 2014. http://knowledge.sagepub.com/view/childmedia/n447.xml
Campbell, Angela J. "Self-Regulation and the Media." *Federal Communications Law Journal*, 1999: 51(3): 711–772. Article 11.
Carey, John, and Martin C. Elton. *When Media Are New: Understanding the Dynamics of New Media Adoption and Use*. Ann Arbor: University of Michigan Press, 2010.
Carr, Nicholas. *The Shallows: What the Internet is Doing to Our Brains*. New York and London: Norton, 2011 [2010].
Center for Internet Addiction. *Internet Addiction Test (IAT)*. 2009. http://netaddiction.com/internet-addiction-test/
Christus Rex. *Pope Urges "fast" from TV during Lent*. 10 March 1996. http://www.christusrex.org/www2/news-old/3-96/es3-10-96.html
Cohen, Stanley. *Folk Devils and Moral Panics*. St. Albans: Paladin, 1973.
Creeber, Glenn, and Royston Martin. *Digital Cultures: Understanding New Media*. Maidenhead: Open University Press, 2009.
Croteau, David, and William Hoynes. *Media/Society: Industry, Images and Audiences*. London: Sage, 2012.
Dahl, Hans Fredrik. *Hallo hallo!: Kringkastingen i Norge, 1920–1940*. Oslo: Cappelen, 1975.
Dawson, Nick. *Being Hal Ashby. Life of a Hollywood Rebel*. Lexington: Kentucky University Press, 2009.
Dewey, John. *The Public and its Problems*. Athens: Ohio University Press, 1991 [1927].
Death Race 2000. Directed by Ron Bartel, 1975.
Disconnect. Directed by Henry A Rubin, 2012.

Drotner, Kirsten. "Dangerous Media? Panic Discourses and Dilemmas of Modernity." *Paedagogica Historica*, 1999: 35(3): 593–619.
Dundjerski, Marina. *Group Gives TV a Cold Reception*. 24 April 1997. http://articles.latimes.com/1997-04-24/entertainment/ca-51886_1_tv-free-america
Enli, Gunn. *Mediated Authenticity: How Media Construct Reality*. New York: Peter Lang, 2015.
Enli, Gunn, Hallvard Moe, Vilde Schanke Sundet, and Trine Syvertsen. "From Fear of Television to Fear for Television: Five Political Debates about New Technologies." *Media History*, 2013: 19(2): 213–227.
Eriksen, Thomas Hylland. *Øyeblikkets tyranni*. Oslo: Aschehoug, 2001.
Evensmo, Sigurd. *Det store tivoli: Film og Kino i Norge*. Oslo: Gyldendal, 1992.
Familie og medier. "Skjermfri uke." *Familie og medier*. 2012. http://fom.no/skjermfri-uke
Fang, Irving. *From Alphabet to Internet: Media in our lives*. New York: Routledge, 2015.
Ferguson, Christopher J., Stephanie M. Rueda, Amanda M. Cruz, Diana Ferguson, Stacey Fritz, and Shawn Smith. "Violent Video Games and Aggression: Causal Relationship or Byproduct of Family Violence and Intrinsic Violence Motivation." *Criminal Justice and Behaviour*, March 2008: 35(3): 311–332.
Ferguson, Christopher J. *Adolescents, Crime and the Media: A Critical Analysis*. New York: Springer, 2013.
The Social Network. Directed by David Fincher, 2010.
Fitzpatrick, Alex. *More Than 40,000 Ultra-Orthodox Jews Hold Rally About Risks of Internet*. 21 May 2012. http://mashable.com/2012/05/21/orthodox-jews-rally-internet/#iYtmpz8Q7qq3
Franzen, Jonathan. "What's Wrong with the Modern World?" *The Guardian*, 9 September 2013.
Freedman, Dan. "Weeklong Television Turnoff aims at 5 Million Viewers." *Tuscaloosa News*, 20 April 1998.
French, Philip, and Julian Petley. *Censoring the Moving Image*. London, New York, Calcutta: Seagull, 2007.
Friedman, Monroe. *Consumer Boycotts: Effecting Change through the Marketplace and the Media*. Routledge: New York and London, 1999.
Gaiman, Neil. "Introduction." In *Fahrenheit 451. 60th Aniversary Edition*, by Ray Bradbury, xi–xvi. New York: Simon and Schuster, 2013.
Garris, Mick. *The Making of David Cronenberg's Videodrome*. n.d. https://www.youtube.com/watch?v=kcKMn3CZ1bk. Uploaded by revok.com 15.1.2010
Geraghty, Lincoln. *American Science Fiction Film and Television*. Oxford and New York: Berg, 2009.
Giddens, Anthony. *Modernity and Self-identity*. Cambridge: Polity, 1991.
Giersing, Morten. *TV i USA*. København: Gyldendal, 1986.

Gilbert, James. *A Cycle of Outrage: America's Reaction to Juvenile Delinquents in the 1950s.* New York: Oxford University Press, 1986.
Gilder, George. *Life after Television: The Coming Transformation of Media and American Life.* New York: Norton, 1992.
Gonzales, Francisco. *Videodrome.* 2013. http://filmconnoisseur.blogspot.no/2013/03/videodrome-1983.html
Gore, Al. *The Assault on Reason.* London: Penguin, 2007.
Grace, Dominick. "From Videodrome to Virtual Light: David Cronenberg and William Gibson." *Extrapolation*, 2003: 44(3): 344–357.
Green, Allan. *Get the F*ck Out Of Social Media – How To Overcome Internet Addiction and Start Living Healthy Life: Internet Addiction, Twitter, Youtube, Social Media.* n/a: Allan Green, 2014.
Grieveson, Lee. *Policing Cinema: Movies and Censorship in Early-Twentieth-Century America.* Berkeley, Los Angeles, London: University of California Press, 2004.
Grynbaum, Michael M. *Ultra-Orthodox Jews Rally to Discuss Risks of Internet.* 20 May 2012. http://www.nytimes.com/2012/05/21/nyregion/ultra-orthodox-jews-hold-rally-on-internet-at-citi-field.html?_r=0
Guins, Raiford. *Edited Clean Version: Technology and the Culture of Control.* Minneapolis: University of Minnesota Press, 2009.
Habermas, Jürgen. *Borgerlig offentlighet.* Lund: Arkiv moderna klassiker, 1984.
Hamerstad, Bjørn Olav, and Johanna Hundvin Almelid. "Et gammeldags liv uten skjermer." *Velsignet helg*, 17 March 2012.
Hannemyr, Gisle. "Begynnelsen på en historie om internett." In *Netts@mfunn*, by Kristin Braa, Per Hetland, and Gunnar Liestøl, 11–28. Oslo: Tano: Ascheoug, 1999.
Heins, Majorie. *Not in Front of the Children: "Indecency", Censorship, and the Innocence of Youth.* New Brunswick, New Jersey and London: Rutgers University Press, 2007.
———. *Sex, Sin and Blasphemy: A Guide to America's Censorship Wars.* New York: New Press, 1993.
Helsper, Ellen J., and Bianca C. Reisdorf. "A Quantitative Examination of Explanations for Reasons for Internet Nonuse." *Cyberpsychology, Behavior, and Social Networking*, 2013: 6(2): 94–99.
Hendy, David. "The Dreadful World of Edwardian Wireless." In *Moral Panics, Social Fears and the Media*, by Siân Nicholas and Tom O'Malley, 76–89. Milton Park, NY: Routledge, 2013.
Heritage, Stuart. "Disconnect: The Internet Thriller that's not Plugged in". *The Guardian*, 6 March 2013.
Herman, Edward S., and Noam Chomsky *Manufacturing Consent: The Political Economy of the Mass Media.* London: The Bodly Head, 1988.

Hertel, Hans. *Verdens litteraturhistorie. Bind 4. 1720–1830.* København: Gyldendal, 1986.

Hilmes, Michele. *Only Connect. A Cultural History of Broadcasting in the United States.* Belmont: Thomson, 2007.

———. *Radio Voices: American Broadcasting, 1922–1952.* Minneapolis: University of Minnesota Press, 1997.

Hirsch, Arthur. *Taking On- and Turning Off.* 26 April 1998. http://articles.baltimoresun.com/1998-04-26/features/1998116062_1_labalme-television-years-south-park

Horkheimer, Max, and Theodor Adorno. "The Culture Industry: Enlightenment as Mass Deception." In *Dialectic of Enlightenment*, by Max Horkheimer and Theodor Adorno, 120–167. London and New York: Verso. 1997 [1944].

Hornig, Susanna. "Digital Delusions: Intelligent Computers in Science Fiction Films." In *Beyond the Stars 3: The Material World in American Popular Film*, by Paul Loukides and Linda Fuller, 207–215. Bowling Green: Bowling Green State University Popular Press, 1993.

Huxley, Aldous. *Brave New World.* New York, London, Toronto, Sydney: Harper Perennial, 2006 [1932].

Illouz, Eva. *Saving the Modern Soul. Therapy, Emotions, and the Culture of Self-Help.* Berkeley: University of California Press, 2008.

Johnson, Carla. *Channel Snubbing Kids Turn On To Other Activities During TV-turnoff Week.* 1 May 1996. http://m.spokesman.com/stories/1996/may/01/channel-snubbing-kids-turn-on-to-other-activities

Johnston, Rich. "Dr Fredric Wertham Lied and Lied And Lied About Comics." *Bleeding Cool.* 2013. http://www.bleedingcool.com/2013/02/11/dr-frederick-wertham-lied-and-lied-and-lied-about-comics/

Her. Directed by Spike Jonze, 2013.

Kant, Immanuel. "What is Enlightenment?" *Modern History Sourcebook.* 1997 [1784]. http://legacy.fordham.edu/halsall/mod/kant-whatis.asp

Karlsen, Faltin. *A World of Excesses. Online Games and Excessive Playing.* Surrey and Burlington: Ashgate, 2013.

Karlsen, Faltin, and Trine Syvertsen. "You can't Smell Roses Online: Intruding Media and Reverse Domestication." *Nordicom Review* 2016: 37 (Special Issue): 25–39. doi:10.1515/nor-2016-0021.

Katz, Elihu, and Paddy Scannell. "The End of Television? Its Impact on the World (So Far)." *The Annals of the American Academy of Political and Social Science*, 2009: 1–236.

Kaufman, Ron. *A Nation of Morons.* 11 October 2007. http://web.archive.org/web/20071011215954/http://turnoffyourtv.com/commentary/morons/stupid.html

Kavka, Misha. *Reality-TV.* Edinburgh: Edinburgh University Press, 2012.

Keane, John. *The Media and Democracy*. Cambridge: Polity, 1991.
Keen, Andrew. *The Cult of the Amateur: How Blogs, MySpace, YouTube, and the Rest of Today's User-Generated Media are Destroying our Economy, Our Culture, and Our Values*. New York: Doubleday, 2008 [2007].
———. "The Second Generation of Internet has Arrived and it's Worse than you Think." In *The Digital Divide*, by av Mark Bauerlein. New York and other: Penguin, 2011.
Kelly, Jim. *He Took The Bet And Lost*. 3 May 1996. http://articles.mcall.com/1996-05-03/news/3093312_tv-turnoff-week-tv-free-america-waddell
King, Carmen Joy. *Facebook Suicide*. 3 October 2008. https://www.adbusters.org/article/facebook-suicide/
King, Geoff, and Tanya Krzywinska. *Science Fiction Cinema: From Outerspace to Cyberspace*. London and New York: Wallflower, 2000.
Kobre, Eytan. "Thou Shalt not Text. Jews Mass at Citi for Exodus from Cyber-Slavery." *New York Post*. 20 May 2012. http://nypost.com/2012/05/20/thou-shalt-not-text/
Kosinski, Jerzy. *Being There*. New York: Grove Press, 1970.
Kraybill, Donald B. "War Against Progress: Coping with Social Change." In *The Amish Struggle With Modernity*, by Donald B. Kraybill and Marc A. Olshan, 35–52. Hanover and London: University Press of New England, 1994.
Krcmar, Marina. *Living Without the Screen: Causes and Consequences of Life Without Television*. New York: Norton, 2009.
Krefting, Ellen, Aina Nøding, and Mona Ringvej. *"En pokkers skrivesyge". 1700-tallets dansk-norske tidsskrifter mellom sensur og ytringsfrihet*. Oslo: Scandinavian Academic Press, 2014.
Kuhn, Anette. *Alien Zone: Cultural Theory and Contemporary Science Fiction Cinema*. London: Verso, 1990.
Leavis, F. R. "Mass Civilization and Minority Culture." In *Cultural Theory and Popular Culture. A Reader*, by av John Storey, 12–19. Harlow: Pearson Education, 2006 [1930].
Lepore, Jill. *The Secret History of Wonder Woman*. New York: Knopf, 2014.
Lessig, Lawrence. *Remix: Making Art and Commerce Thrive in the Hybrid Economy*. New York: Penguin, 2008.
Lewis, Tom. "Legislating Morality: Victorian and Modern Legal Responses to Pornography." In *Behaving Badly: Social Panic and Moral Outrage – Victorian and Modern Parallels*, by Judith Rowbotham and Kim Stevenson, 143–158. Aldershot: Ashgate, 2003.
Liestøl, Gunnar. "Fra Memex til World Wide Web." In *Medier, påvirkning og samfunn*, by Berit von der Lippe and Odd Nordhaug, 533–551. Oslo: Cappelen Akademisk, 1999.
Lippmann, Walter. "Public Opinion." *Project Gutenberg*. 2002 [1922]. http://www.gutenberg.org/cache/epub/6456/pg6456-images.html

Loukides, Paul. "Introduction. Plot Conventions in American Popular Film." In *Beyond the Stars 2: Plot Conventions in American Film*, by Paul Loukides and Linda Fuller, 1–5. Bowling Green: Bowling Green State University Popular Press, 1991.

Loukides, Paul, and Linda Fuller. "Introduction. Conventions of the Material World in Popular Film." In *Beyond the Stars 3: The Material World in American Popular Film*, by Paul Loukides and Linda Fuller, 1–4. Bowling Green: Bowling Green State University Popular Press, 1993.

Network. Directed by Sidney Lumet, 1976.

Macdonald, Dwight. *Masscult and Midcult: Essays Against the American Grain*. New York: New York Review of Books, 2011 [1960].

Madsen, Ole Jacob. *Den terapeutiske kultur*. Oslo: Universitetsforlaget, 2010.

———. *Det er innover vi må gå*. Oslo: Universitetsforlaget, 2014.

Mander, Jerry. *Four Arguments for the Elimination of Television*. New York: Morrow, 1978 [1977].

Marvin, Carolyn. *When Old Technologies Were New*. New York and Oxford: Oxford University Press, 1988.

Mathews, Tom D. *Censored: The Story of Film Censorship in Britain*. London: Chatto and Windus, 1994.

Maushart, Susan. *The Winter of Our Disconnect: How Three Totally Wired Teenagers (and a Mother Who Slept with Her iPhone) Pulled the Plug on Their Technology and Lived to Tell the Tale*. New York: Penguin, 2010.

McAlister, Nancy. *For 7 days, TV's a Turnoff*. 22 April 1999. http://jacksonville.com/tu-online/stories/042299/ent_S0422Tur.html

McGee, Micki. *Self-help Inc: Makeover Culture in American Life*. Oxford Scholarship online: May 2012. doi: 10.1093/acprof:oso/9780195171242.001.0001, 2005.

McGrane, Bernard, and John Gunderson. *Watching TV Is Not Required: Thinking About Media and Thinking About Thinking*. New York: Routledge, 2010.

McKee, Alan. *Wall to Wall*. 6 October 2006. http://flowtv.org/2006/10/dallas-dvd-populism-quality-television/

McLuhan, Marshall. *Understanding Media: The Extension of Man*. London: Sphere books, 1968 [1964].

McNair, Brian. *Journalists in Film. Heroes and Villains*. Edinburgh: Edinburgh University Press, 2010.

McRobbie, Angela. "The Moral Panic in the Age of the Postmodern Mass Media." In *Postmodernism and Popular Culture*, by Angela McRobbie, 177–197. London: Routledge, 1994.

Menand, Louis. "Introduction." In *Masscult and Midcult*, by Dwight MacDonald, vii–xxii. New York: New York Review Books, 2011.

Meyrowitz, Joshua. *No Sense of Place*. New York, Oxford: Oxford University Press, 1985.

Miller, Paul. *Against the Future: Inside the Jewish Anti-Internet Rally.* 22 May 2012. http://www.theverge.com/2012/5/22/3035274/against-the-future-inside-the-jewish-anti-internet-rally
———. *I'm Still Here: Back Online After a Year Without the Internet.* 1 May 2013. http://www.theverge.com/2013/5/1/4279674/im-still-here-back-online-after-a-year-without-the-internet
Minow, Newton N. "'Television and the Public Interest'. Speech on May 9th, 1961 to National Association of Broadcasters, Washington, DC." *American Rhetoric.* 1961. http://www.americanrhetoric.com/speeches/newtonminow.htm
Modleski, Tania. "The terror of pleasure: The contemporary horror film and post-modern theory". In *The Film Cultures Reader*, by Graeme Turner, 268–275. London: Routledge, 2002.
Morozov, Evgeny. *The Net Delusion: The Dark Side of Internet Freedom.* New York: Public Affairs, 2011.
Mz. *God TV-fri Påske.* 7 April 2006. http://www.dagen.no/Innenriks/God_TV-fri_p%C3%A5ske-34446
Natale, Simone, and Gabriele Balbi. "Media and the Imaginary in History." *Media History*, 2014: 20(2): 203–218.
National Film Preservation Board. *Film Registry.* 2015. https://www.loc.gov/programs/national-film-preservation-board/film-registry/descriptions-and-essays/
Negroponte, Nicholas. *Being Digital.* New York: Vintage, 1995.
Newcomb, Lori Humphrey. *Reading Popular Romance in Early Modern England.* New York: Columbia University Press, 2002.
S1m0ne. Directed by Andrew Niccol, 2002.
Nicholas, Siân, and Tom O'Malley. *Moral Panics, Social Fears and the Media.* Milton Park, NY: Routledge, 2013.
Nymo, Tanja Pedersen. *Slibrige scener, listige knep.* MA-thesis, Oslo: University of Oslo, 2002.
O'Reilly, Tim. "What is Web 2.0: Design Patterns and Business Models for the Next Generation of Software." In *The Digital Divide*, by Mark Bauerlein. London: Penguin, 2011 [2005].
Orwell, George. *Nineteen Eighty-Four.* London: Penguin, 2008 [1949].
Parisier, Eli. *The Filter Bubble: What the Internet is Hiding From You.* London: Penguin, 2011.
Pearson, Geoffrey. "Falling Standards: A Short, Sharp History of Moral Decline." In *Video Nasties: Freedom and Censorship in the Media*, by Martin Barker, 88–103. London: Pluto, 1984.
Phillips, Kendall R. *Controversial Cinema: Films that Outraged America.* Westport: Praeger, 2008.
Pierce, Charles P. *Idiot America – How Stupidity Became a Virtue in the Land of the Free.* New York: Anchor Books, 2010.

Plato. *Plato, The Phaedrus, a Dialogue Between Socrates and Phaedrus Recorded by Plato.* Around 370 BC. http://www.units.miamioh.edu/technologyandhumanities/plato.htm

Portwood-Stacer, Laura. "Media Refusal and Conspicuous Non-Consumption: The Performative and Political Dimensions of Facebook Abstention." *New Media and Society*, December 2012: 15(7): 1041–1057.

Postman, Andrew. "Introduction." In *Amusing Ourselves to Death*, by Neil Postman, vii–xvi. London: Penguin, 2005b.

Postman, Neil. *Amusing Ourselves to Death.* London: Penguin, 2005a [1985].

I, Robot. Directed by Alex Proyas. 2004.

Putnham, Robert D. *Bowling Alone: The Collapse and Revival of American Community.* New York: Simon and Schuster, 2000.

Randall, Adrian. "Reinterpreting 'Luddism': Resistance to New Technology in the British Industrial Revolution." In *Resistance to New Technology*, by Martin Bauer, 57–80. Cambridge: Cambridge University Press, 1995.

Ravatn, Agnes. *Operasjon sjølvdisiplin.* Oslo: Samlaget, 2014.

Reading, Anna. "Campaigns to Change the Media." In *The Media in Britain*, by Jane Stokes and Anna Reading, 170–183. Basingstoke: Macmillan, 1999.

The Quiz Show. Directed by Robert Redford, 1994.

Refsnes, Ingeborg. "TV-fri uke i Melhus." *Adresseavisa*, 24 January 2006.

Reibman, James E. "Introduction." In *Seduction of the Innocent*, by Fredric Wertham, v–xliv. New York: Main Road Books, 2004.

Reisdorf, Bianca Christin. "Non-Adoption of the Internet in Great Britain and Sweden." *Information, Communication and Society*, 2011: 14(3): 400–420.

Reith, John. *Broadcast Over Britain.* London: Hodder and Stoughton, 1924.

Rheingold, Howard. *The Virtual Community: Homesteading on the Electronic Frontier.* New York: Harper Perennial, 1993.

Robertson, James. *The Hidden Cinema. British Film Censorship 1913–1972.* London: Routledge, 1989.

Rogers, Everett M. *Diffusions of Innovations.* New York: The Free Press, 1995 [1962].

Rommetveit, Ingrid, and Anne-Lise With. "Tematisk analyse som balansekunst." In *Filmanalytiske tradisjoner*, by Eva Bakøy and Jo Sondre Moseng, 107–113. Oslo: Universitetsforlaget, 2008.

Rosen, Christine. "The Age of Egocasting." *The New Atlantis*, 2004: Fall 2004–Winter 2005.

Rosenwein, Barbara H. "Worrying About Emotions in History." *The American Historical Review*, 2002: 107(3): 821–845.

The Hunger Games. Directed by Gary Ross, 2012.

Rothman, David. *Ray Bradbury on Fahrenheit 451: "I Wasn't Worried About Censorship—I was Worried about People Being Turned into Morons by TV".* 4 June 2007. http://teleread.com/ray-bradbury-on-fahrenheit-451-i-wasnt-worried-about-censorship-i-was-worried-about-books-being-turned-into-morons-by-tv/

Rowbotham, Judith, and Kim Stevenson. *Behaving Badly: Social Panic and Moral Outrage – Victorian and Modern Paralells*. Aldershot: Ashgate, 2003.

Scannell, Paddy. *Media and Communication*. London: Sage, 2007.

Scannel, Paddy, and David Cardiff. *A Social History of British Broadcasting. Vol. 1: 1922–1939: Serving the Nation*, Oxford: Blackwell, 1991.

Trust. Directed by David Schwimmer, 2010.

Screen-Free week. *History of SFW*. 2014. http://www.screenfree.org/wp-content/uploads/2014/04/HistoryOfSFW.pdf

———. *Spread the Word*. 2016a. http://www.screenfree.org/spread-the-word/

———. *What is SFW*. 2016b. http://www.screenfree.org/basics/

Selwyn, Neil. "Apart from Technology: Understanding People's Non-Use of Information and Communication Technologies in Everyday Life." *Technology in Society*, 2003: 25: 99–116.

Shirky, Clay. *Cognitive Surplus: How Technology Makes Consumers into Collaborators*. New York: Penguin, 2010.

Shulins, Nancy. "Tips for foreldre som vil endre sine TV-vaner." NTB, 03 December 1987.

Singer, Stacey. *Week Turns Kids On To Turning Off*. 25 April 1996. http://articles.chicagotribune.com/1996-04-25/news/9604250110_1_henry-labalme-tv-free-america-matt-pawa

Smith, Anthony, and Richard Paterson. *Television: An International History*. Oxford: Oxford University Press, 1998.

Smith-Isaksen, Marthe, and Vegard Higraff. *Videovold: Regulering av videomediet 1980–2004*. Oslo: Statens filmtilsyn, 2004.

Solomon, Robert, and Kathleen Higgins. *A Short History of Philosophy*. Oxford: Oxford University Press, 1996.

St.tid 1954. Interpellasjon fra Wikborg om dårlige tegneserier mv. 507–518 (Norwegian Parliament, 3 March 1954).

St.tid 1957. Om innføring av fjernsyn i Norge. 2447–2478 (Norwegian Parliament, 25 June 1957).

Stein, Micah. *Yiddish, Translated on a Jumbotron*. 21 May 2012. http://www.tabletmag.com/scroll/100241/yiddish-translated-on-a-jumbotron

Storey, John. *Cultural Theory and Popular Culture*. Harlow: Pearson Longman, 2009.

Stulen, Hege. "En uke uten skjermbilde." *Sandefjords blad*, 28 April 2005.

Sundet, Vilde Schanke. "Making Sense of Mobile Media." PhD-thesis, University of Oslo, Oslo, 2012.

Sundin, Jan, and Sam Willner. *Social Change and Health in Sweden*. Solna: Institute of Public Health, 2007.

Sutter, Gavin. "Penny Dreadfuls and Perverse Domains: Victorian and Modern Moral Panics." In *Behaving Badly: Social Panics and Moral Outrage: Victorian and Modern Paralells*, by Judith Rowbotham and Kim Stevenson, 159–176. Aldershot: Ashgate, 2003.

Swales, Martin. *Goethe: The Sorrows of Young Werther*. Cambridge: Cambridge University Press, 1987.
Syvertsen, Trine, Gunn Enli, Ole Mjøs, and Hallvard Moe. *The Media Welfare State. Nordic Media in the Digital Era*. Michigan: University of Michigan Press, 2014.
Sørensen, Tone. *Vil unngå nett-overgrep mot barn*. 17 March 2010. http://www.blv.no/lokalsider/sortland/article5027753.ece
Tennant, Kyle. *Unfriend Yourself: Three Days to Discern, Detox and Decide about Social Media*. Chicago: Moody, 2012.
Thompson, Kristin, and David Bordwell. *Film History: An Introduction. International Edition*. Boston: McGraw Hill, 2010.
Tracey, Michael, and David Morrison. *Whitehouse*. London: MacMillan, 1979.
Turkle, Sherry. *Alone Together: Why We Expect More from Technology and Less from Each Other*. New York: Basic Books, 2011.
———. *Life on the Screen: Identity in the Age of the Internet*. New York: Simon and Schuster, 1995.
TV Turnoff. *About Us*. 6 August 2002a. http://web.archive.org/web/20020806195313/http://www.tvturnoff.org/aboutus.htm
———. *Allies*. 6 October 2002e. http://web.archive.org/web/20021006183245/http://tvturnoff.org/tvtowallies.htm
———. *Are you Ready for TV Turnoff Week?* 18 August 2000c. http://web.archive.org/web/20000818231310/http://www.tvturnoff.org/ArticlesPage4.htm
———. *International TV-Turnoff*. 4 October 2002d. http://web.archive.org/web/20021004025015/http://tvturnoff.org/international.htm
———. *Surgeon General: Watch less TV*. 18 August 2000b. http://web.archive.org/web/20000818231304/http:/tvturnoff.org/ArticlesPage2.htm
———. *TV Turnoff*. 7 June 2002c. http://web.archive.org/web/20020607135840/http://turnoffyourtv.com/TV.turnoff.week.html
———. *TV Turnoff Network*. 16 August 2000a. http://web.archive.org/web/20000816033801/http://www.tvturnoff.org/StaffPage.htm
———. *TV Turnoff Week*. 7 August 2002b. http://www.tvturnoff.org/orgweek.htm
———. *TV Turnoff Week*. 31 August 2012. http://web.archive.org/web/20120831033954/http:/www.turnoffyourtv.com/turnoffweek/TV.turnoff.week.html
Tvinnereim, Audun. *Triviallitteraturen og skolen*. Bergen: Universitetsforlaget, 1978.
Ulveseth, Kari. "Ja til skjermfrihet." *Adresseavisen*, 30 April 2005: 31.
vanZonen, Lisbeth, and Minna Aslama. "Understanding Big Brother: An Analysis of Current Research." *Javnost*, 2006: 13(2): 85–96.
Vint, Cherryl, and Mark Bould. "All that Melts into Air is Solid: Rematerialising Capital in Cube and Videodrome." *Socialism and Democracy*, 2006: 20(3): 217–243.

Vitka, William. *GameSpeak: Jack Thompson.* 24 February 2005. http://www.cbsnews.com/news/gamespeak-jack-thompson/
Ward, Ken. *Mass Communication and the Modern World.* Basingstoke and London: MacMillan, 1989.
The Truman Show. Directed by Peter Weir, 1998.
Wertham, Fredric. *Seduction of the Innocent.* New York: Main Road Books, 2004 [1954].
White dot. *About Us.* 2000b. http://www.whitedot.org/issue/fix_aboutus.asp
———. *Britain Ignores White Dot Endorsement.* 2015. http://www.whitedot.org/issue/iss_front.asp
———. *FAQS.* 2000a. http://www.whitedot.org/issue/fix_faqs.asp
———. *Get Out of the Box.* 21 April 2009. https://jagadees.wordpress.com/2009/04/21/tv-free-life/
Whitehouse, Mary. *Cleaning up TV. From Protest to Participation.* London: Blandford Press, 1967.
———. *Quite Contrary. An Autobiography.* London: Pan Books, 1993.
Williams, Kevin. "Moral Panics, Emotion and Newspaper History." In *Moral Panics, Social Fears and the Media. Historical Perspectives*, by Siân Nicholas and Tom O'Malley, 28–45. Milton Park, NY: Routledge, 2013.
Williams, Raymond. *Culture and Society, 1780–1950.* New York: Columbia University Press, 1958.
———. *Television: Technology and Cultural Form.* London: Routledge, 2008 [1974].
Winn, Marie. *The Plug-In Drug.* New York: Bantham, 1980 [1977].
———. *The Plug-In Drug: Television, Computers, and Family Life.* New York: Penguin, 2002.
———. *Unplugging the Plug-in-Drug: The "NO TV Week" Guide.* New York: Penguin, 1987.
Wolfe, Kenneth M. *The Churches and the British Broadcasting Corporation.* London: SCM Press, 1984.
Woodstock, L. "Media Resistance: Opportunities for Practice Theory and New Media Research." *International Journal of Communication*, 2014: 8: 1983–2001.
Worland, Rick. *The Horror Film: An Introduction.* Oxford: Blackwell, 2007.
Wyatt, S., G. Thomas, and T. Terranova. "They Came, They Surfed, They Went Back to the Beach: Conceptualizing Use and Non-Use of the Internet." In *Virtual Society: Technology, Cyberpole, Reality*, by S. Woolgar, 23–40. Oxford: Oxford University Press, 2002.
Wyatt, Sally. "Non-Users also Matter: The Construction of Users and Non-Users of the Internet." In *How Users Matter: The Co-Construction of Users and Technologies*, by Nelly Oudshoorn and Trevor Pinch, 67–80. Cambridge, MA: The MIT Press, 2003.

Y'Gasset, Ortega. *The Revolt of the Masses*. New York and London: Norton, 1993 [1930].

Young, Kimberly. *Caught in the Net: How to Recognize the Signs of Internet Addiction and a Winning Strategy for Recovery*. New York: John Wiley and Sons, 1998.

——. *Tangled in the Web: Understanding Cybersex from Fantasy to Addiction*. n/a: 1st Books, 2000.

Ytreberg, Espen. "Det ekspanderende selvet. Om deltakelse i reality-TV." *Vinduet*, 2003.

——. *Hva er medievitenskap*. Oslo: Universitetsforlaget, 2008.

Zane, Mark. *Social Media Addiction. How to Reclaim Your Life from Facebook*. n/a: Mark Zane, 2014.

Öhman, Anders. *Populärlitteratur: De poulära genrernas estetik och historia*. Lund: Studentlitteratur, 2002.

Index

A
Action, forms of, 3, 13–14, 75–76, 79, 96–97, 125–127, 128
Adbusters, 57, 66, 70, 93
Adorno, Theodore W., 25, 29, 48, 55–56
Alone together, 85, 113, 124
  See also Metaphors in media resistance
Ambiguity, 9, 16
  See also Emotions in media resistance
Amish, 10
Anders, Günter, 60, 61
Artificial intelligence, 110
Ashby, Hal, 101, 102
Authenticity, 89, 96, 103, 114, 116, 129
Authoritarian regimes, 43, 85, 96

B
Being there, 8, 100–104, 112–116
Bellamy, Edward, 35
Big brother, reality show, 42, 106
Blade Runner, 104, 110
Book people, 52–53
Books, 16–18, 22, 25, 31, 36, 40, 43–46, 48–53, 58, 61, 62, 64, 65, 71, 74, 75, 79–81, 84–87, 89, 91, 92, 101, 103, 111, 120, 122, 123–125, 130
Books, abbreviated, 48
Boycott, 22, 65, 75, 96, 126
  See also Action, forms of
Brave new world, 7, 36, 38, 39, 44, 46–49, 51, 52, 56, 59, 61, 100, 107, 114, 123, 130
Britain, 8, 14, 20, 27, 41, 57, 58, 70, 71, 73
British Broadcasting Corporation (BBC), 24, 57, 58

C
Cable, 100, 103, 112
Campaigns, 3, 4, 22, 23, 26, 27, 32, 36, 56–59, 68, 69, 73, 75, 93, 94, 106, 125
  See also Action, forms of
Carr, Nicholas, 79, 81, 83, 84, 86, 87
Caught in the net, 77–97, 121
  See also Metaphors in media resistance
Cell phones, 85, 109
Censorship, 3–5, 8, 13, 17, 22–23, 27, 28, 31–32, 43, 61, 68, 125
  See also Action, forms of

Church, resistance of, 4, 16–18, 22, 24, 31, 32, 58, 69, 73, 96, 126
Cinema, 5, 11, 16, 21, 22, 27, 30
Civilization, threats to, 27, 29, 33, 36, 43, 48, 49, 52, 53, 64, 102, 103, 123
Comics, 11, 16, 25–28, 32, 37, 46, 48, 58, 73, 120–122
Comics code, 27
Commercialization, 8, 24, 25, 44, 47, 57, 60, 62, 63, 70, 73, 107, 108, 121, 123, 126
Community, 5, 11, 16, 28, 30, 31, 35, 38, 45–47, 49, 56, 61, 63, 64, 68, 69, 71, 75, 77, 79, 81, 84, 87, 88, 90, 95, 101, 112, 113, 120, 123, 124
  See also Values and concerns in media resistance
Conversation, 2, 39, 66, 79, 86–89, 96, 109, 120, 124, 126–128
Copycat effect, 26, 120
Couch potato, 56, 73, 95, 122
  See also Metaphors in media resistance
Cronenberg, David, 103–105
Cultural pessimism, 9, 67, 128
Culture, 2–5, 7, 8, 12, 16, 17, 19, 22–25, 27–31, 35–38, 40, 42–44, 46–50, 56, 60–62, 69, 71, 73, 79, 83, 92, 95, 101–103, 105, 107, 111, 112, 120–123, 125, 126, 130
  See also Values and concerns in media resistance
Cyberpunk, 104

D

Death Race 2000, 106
Democracy, 5, 12, 16, 23, 24, 27, 28, 31, 35, 38, 46, 47, 49, 50, 56, 60, 61, 64, 74, 77–79, 82, 88, 90, 95, 96, 101, 112, 115, 120, 123
  See also Values and concerns in media resistance
Detox, 13, 14, 77–97, 125–127
  See also Action, forms of; Fasting; Media abstention
Dewey, John, 12, 31
Dictatorship of idiots, 83, 121
  See also Metaphors in media resistance
Diffusion theory, 6, 72
  See also Laggards
Digital television, 72
Disappointment, 8, 9, 26, 28–30, 57, 59, 73, 74, 77–97, 121, 123, 128, 129
  See also Emotions in media resistance
Disconnect, 8, 100, 108–111, 113–116, 124
Doctors, resistance of, 27
Doomsday, 7–8, 35–36, 99–100, 123
Dystopia, 36, 43, 46, 51, 62, 74, 112
Dystopian fiction, 8, 35–53, 85, 96, 128
Dystopian film, 13, 99–117

E

Echo chamber, 85, 123
  See also Metaphors in media resistance
Educational professions, resistance of, 13, 75
  See also Teachers, resistance of
Education for crime, 21–23, 121
  See also Metaphors in media resistance
Education for terror, 28, 121
  See also Metaphors in media resistance

Ego-casting, 85, 123
  See also Metaphors in media resistance
Emotions in media resistance, 128
Enlightenment, 5, 8, 12, 16, 18, 20, 22, 27–31, 38, 40, 46, 47, 49, 50, 56, 62, 64, 73, 79, 82, 84, 88, 90, 95, 101, 112, 120, 122, 123, 126
  See also Values and concerns in media resistance
Epidemics, 20, 30, 88, 124, 125
  See also Metaphors in media resistance
Eriksen, Thomas Hylland, 78, 86
Escapism, 12, 20, 42, 49

F
Facebook, 10, 90, 94, 108
Fahrenheit 451, 8, 36, 43–48, 50–53, 56, 59, 68, 100, 107, 114, 123, 130
Fasting, 13, 79, 96, 125, 127
  See also Action, form of; Detox; Media abstention
Fear, 4, 5, 9, 23, 49, 57, 68, 95, 108, 128
  See also Emotions in media resistance
Feely, feelies, 38–41, 47
Filter bubble, 85, 123
  See also Metaphors in media resistance
Frankfurt school, 25
Franzen, Jonathan, 6, 119–120

G
Games, 10, 38, 41, 58, 60, 80, 91, 111, 121, 124
Garbage, 20, 121
  See also Metaphors in media resistance
Goethe, 18
Gore, Al, 8, 78, 103, 104

H
Hamlet, 46, 48
  See also Shakespeare, William
Health, 5, 12, 20, 21, 28, 30, 31, 44, 46, 49, 56, 61, 63, 74, 79, 81, 82, 90, 101, 114, 119, 120, 124, 125
  See also Values and concerns in media resistance
Her, 8, 100, 108, 110–114, 124
High culture, 27, 29, 37, 48, 95, 122
Hope, 13, 38, 51–53, 65, 77–78, 84, 86, 96, 101, 114–116, 123, 127–129
  See also Emotions in media resistance
Horkheimer, Max, 25, 29, 48, 55–56
Horror, 19, 25–28, 70, 104
Humanities, threat to, 2, 51, 52, 120, 123, 128
Hunger Games, The, 106
Huxley, Aldous, 36–38, 40, 46, 51, 61, 74, 82
Hysteria, 4, 5, 9, 21
  See also Emotions in media resistance

I
The idiot box, 12, 56, 121
  See also Metaphors in media resistance
Infestation, 20
  See also Metaphors in media resistance
I, Robot, 110

J

Jewish, 26, 87
Jonze, Spike, 110
Jugglers brain, 84, 96, 122
   See also Metaphors in media resistance

K

Keen, Andrew, 79, 81, 82–83, 86, 121

L

Laggards, 4–7, 96, 126
   See also Diffusion theory
Librarians, resistance of, 20, 27, 65, 66, 68
Lowest common denominator, 60, 121
   See also Metaphors in media resistance
Luddites, 4–7, 56, 67, 75, 86, 96, 126

M

Macbeth, 27
   See also Shakespeare, William
Mander, Jerry, 56, 59–64, 66, 74, 75, 100
Manufacture consent, 12, 107
Mass culture, 30, 37, 38, 43, 46–48, 107, 121, 122
   See also High culture
Matrix, The, 104
McLuhan, Marshall, 4, 60, 61–63, 105
Media abstention, 13, 14, 79, 90, 97
   See also Action, forms of; Detox; Fasting
Media panic, 2, 4, 8, 103, 121
   See also Moral panic

Media prophesies, warnings, 101, 112
Media regulation, 14, 95
Media resistance, explanation, 9–11
Media studies, 2, 13, 60, 71, 74, 120, 129
Media Welfare State, 8
Medical professions, resistance of, 20, 32, 127
Medium theory, 13, 60
Metaphors in media resistance, 7, 12, 18, 80, 120–125
Moralists, 4–7, 56, 59, 75, 96, 126, 130
Morality, 5, 12, 16, 24, 28, 29, 31, 38, 46, 47, 49, 56, 58, 79, 80–82, 88, 90, 101, 113, 114, 120–122, 126
   See also Values and concerns in media resistance
Moral panic, 4, 74, 116, 121
   See also Media panic
Morozov, Evgeny, 85, 86
Murder simulators, 80, 121
   See also Metaphors in media resistance
Music, 22, 24, 35, 38–40, 42, 83, 91, 94, 104, 110, 111

N

Nazi Germany, 24–25
Network, 13, 19, 24, 32, 60, 66, 67, 70, 71, 73, 83, 100, 101, 103, 109
Nineteen Eighty-Four, 8, 36, 41–43, 47–49, 51, 52, 56, 59, 84, 100, 107, 114, 123, 130
Non-use, 7
   See also Media abstention
Nordic countries, 8, 70
   See also Scandinavia

Norway, 1, 22, 28, 32, 62, 70–71, 91, 93
Novels, resistance to, 48

O
Office of Radio Research, 33
Online media, 79, 80, 82, 85, 87, 89–92, 95, 96, 100, 108, 109, 112, 114, 116, 120, 122, 124, 126, 127
Oral communication, 31
Orwell, George, 36, 37, 43, 46, 51, 61, 68, 82–85
Othello, 40
  See also Shakespeare, William

P
Passivity, passive media consumption, 1, 39, 74, 95, 122, 125
Penny dreadfuls, 12, 19
  See also Metaphors in media resistance
Plato, 17
The Plug-In-Drug, 63–65, 81, 102, 125
  See also Metaphors in media resistance
Poison, 20
  See also Metaphors in media resistance
Pornography, 38, 40, 43, 47, 58, 80–82, 88, 90, 95
Postman, Neil, 56, 61–66, 72, 74, 75, 84, 91, 100, 102, 126
Print media, resistance to, 18
Print vs screen, 46–48

Professional media resistance, 19, 88, 104
Progressives, 7, 22, 30, 31, 112, 121, 128
Prohibition, 13, 32
  See also Action, forms of
Propaganda, 12, 25, 30, 39, 40, 43, 46, 47, 49, 50, 52, 96, 123
Psychologists, psychiatrists, resistance of, 21, 25, 27, 80
Pulp fiction, 19
  See also Metaphors in media resistance

Q
Quiz show, The, 102

R
Radio, 11, 16, 23–25, 31–33, 37–39, 41, 45, 47, 56, 57, 78, 105, 107, 113, 122–124
Reading, 17–20, 26, 27, 40, 44, 48, 64, 71, 84, 91, 95, 122–124, 130
Reality television, 100, 106
Reith, John, 24
Religious resistance, 75, 88, 127
Resistance literature, 56, 79, 93
Rubin, Henry Alex, 108

S
S1m0ne, 110
Scandinavia, 8, 14, 16, 57, 62, 70, 79, 125, 127
  See also Nordic countries

Science fiction, 19, 36, 100, 104, 110, 112
Scientists, resistance of, 26, 27, 51, 52, 66
Screen-free week, 72–73, 92–94
Seashell radio, 45, 47
Self-help, 14, 89–92, 96, 126–128
Self-reflexivity among resisters, 9, 96, 126
Serial fiction, 19–20, 37
Serial literature, 16, 20, 73
Sex, 25, 38, 42, 46, 47, 57, 80, 103, 108, 113, 116, 121
Shakespeare, William, 27, 40, 43, 48, 52, 107
Social media, 2, 11, 78, 79, 86, 87, 89, 90, 94–97, 108–110, 114, 120–124, 126
Social network, The, 108
Socrates, 17
Sorrows of Young Werther, 18
Stern, Andrew, 108

T
Taliban, 10, 71
Tangled in the web, 80, 81, 121
  See also Metaphors in media resistance
Teachers, resistance of, 20, 22, 27, 51, 65, 68, 70, 81
Techies, resistance of, 13, 80, 81, 127
Technology studies, 4
Technophobia, 2, 4
Telescreen, 41–43, 47
Television, 1, 2, 10, 11, 28, 37–39, 42–47, 55–67, 69–76, 77–79, 81, 83, 84, 87, 88, 91–93, 95, 96, 100–106, 108, 109, 112–116, 120–126, 129, 130
Trash, 22, 40

  See also Metaphors in media resistance
Truman Show, The, 8, 42, 100, 106–108, 116
Trust, 108
Turkle, Sherry, 78, 79, 81, 83–86, 91, 113, 124
TV-Free America, 57, 65–70, 73, 92
TV-turnoff week, 56, 57, 66, 68–72, 74, 75, 92
Twitter, 6, 88

U
US, USA, 8, 14, 15–16, 19, 20, 22–27, 31, 32, 56, 57, 59, 60, 65, 69, 71, 73, 75, 77–80, 93, 104, 125, 126, 127

V
Values and concerns in media resistance, 11–12, 37, 46–48, 56, 73–74, 89, 95–96, 112–114, 120–125
Victorian era, 5
Victorian morality, 29
Victorian values, 29
Videodrome, 8, 100, 103–105, 109, 112–116
Video nasties, 59, 105
  See also Metaphors in media resistance

W
Wall-to-Wall Dallas, 121
  See also Metaphors in media resistance
Weir, Peter, 106

Wertham, Fredric, 25–28, 32, 126
White dot, 57, 66, 71–73, 92
Whitehouse, Mary, 56–59, 64, 73, 75, 100
Wikborg, Erling, 26, 28
Wikipedia, 61, 72, 82
Winn, Marie, 10, 56, 63–68, 75, 81, 86, 102, 126
Women, vulnerable to media influence, 48
Writing diarrhoea, 18, 121, 125
See also Metaphors in media resistance
Writing epidemic, 18
See also Metaphors in media resistance

Y
Young, Kimberly, 78–81, 121
Young people, vulnerable to media influence, 20, 21, 120
Youtube, 82

The manufacturer's authorised representative in the EU is Springer Nature Customer Service Centre GmbH, Europaplatz 3, 69115 Heidelberg, Germany. If you have any concerns regarding our products, please contact ProductSafety@springernature.com

Printed and bound by CPI Group (UK) Ltd, Croydon, CR0 4YY
23/03/2026
02076402-0007